HEAVEN OR HELL?

THIS IS THE END!

by

DAVID ALLAN SILVA

Copyright © 2019 David Allan Silva
The Great End Time Commission Ministry

All rights reserved. No portion of this book may be reproduced, stored in a retrieval system, or transmitted in any form or by any means – electronic, mechanical, photocopy, recording, scanning, or other – except for brief quotations in critical reviews or articles, without the prior written permission of the publisher.

Unless otherwise noted, Scripture quotations are taken from the Holy Bible, New Living Translation, NLT copyright 1996, 2004, 2007, 2013 by Tyndale House Foundation. Used by permission of Tyndale House Publishers, Inc., Carol Stream, Illinois 60188. All rights reserved. Scripture quotations noted as KJV are taken from the King James Version, KJV King James Version, public domain.

Cover photo is courtesy of Shutterstock and is used by permission.

E-Mail the author at thebloodofjesussavesall@gmail.com
Heaven or Hell? This is the End!
David Allan Silva, Author
Carlene Ann Silva, Editor
Heaven's Stairs by Sharilee Rudolph

DEDICATED TO MY FATHER GOD YAHWEH,

MY LORD AND SAVIOR JESUS CHRIST,

AND THE HOLY SPIRIT

TO MY WIFE, TO MY CHILDREN, TO MY

FAMILY, TO MY FRIENDS, AND TO MY

MENTORS WHO HAVE GUIDED ME THROUGH

MY WALK OF FAITH

CONTENTS

Introduction	
One	THE BEGINNING
	I WAS TAKEN UP TO HEAVEN
Two	STUDYING GOD'S WORD
Three	I WAS TAKEN DOWN TO HELL!
Four	WORLD HISTORY IS FOUND IN THE BIBLE
Five	THE SCIENCE OF GOD
Six	THE ATTACKS FROM SATAN AND THE MIRACLES OF MY LIFE
Seven	THE WAR OF THE MIND
Eight	THE TRUTH ABOUT THE SUPERNATURAL
Nine	THE PROPHECIES OF JESUS CHRIST FOUND IN THE BIBLE
Ten	LIFE IS ALL ABOUT LOVE
Eleven	THIS IS THE END
Twelve	MY FINAL THOUGHTS

INTRODUCTION

Greetings to all my brothers and sisters all over the world, loved by God, called to be saints. Grace and peace to you from God our Father and our Savior the Lord Jesus Christ. I plead the Blood of Jesus over you for protection from the evil one, Satan. My name is David Allan Silva. I have been given the honor to serve my God and Savior Jesus Christ, by sharing with you, secret and hidden things that the Lord himself has made known to me during my lifetime. In the summer of 2018, the Lord woke me very early one morning at about 4 am, and I felt in my spirit that I was to get up and start to write this book. He was "telling" me that it was time to share with the people of the world, everything He had shown me over my lifetime regarding the last days – the days we are now living in.

I don't hear His audible voice. When the Lord communicates with me, He gives me a thought or thoughts. He will either put a word or a scripture verse in my mind, and then I look for the word or verse in the Bible. Once I find and read it in the Bible, He reveals what He wants to "say" or convey to me. The Bible is my main source of information. He does the same thing to teach me about things of the natural world. Once I "hear" or find out what He is trying to teach me, He will confirm it with me. Almost on a daily basis, He conveys something to me. I also receive information through dreams about events that are yet to happen. Sometimes when He gives me a thought, almost immediately He will reveal its meaning. Let me give you an example. I might be thinking about lyrics of a particular Christian song, and five minutes later when I get in my car and turn on the radio, that song is playing. He is using those words to "speak" to me. It's probably happened to you. Sometimes He uses the news on television, or He will direct me to a certain documentary to reveal something to me. Through this book, I will share with you what the Lord has revealed to me.

I pray that you will read this book it in its entirety, searching out the facts for yourself. I see things in this world in black or white, right or wrong, good versus evil. The Lord made me this way, and I find no gray areas when it comes to God's Word.

You need to understand that this book is based on actual events that I have experienced throughout my life and is backed up by His Holy Word, the Bible. Don't take my word for it. I will provide Bible verses and other evidence to support statements that I make. It tells us in Revelation 12:11, *And they have defeated him* (Satan) *by the blood of the Lamb* (Jesus Christ) *and by their testimony. And they did not love their lives so much that they were afraid to die.* This book is my testimony. The Lord has given me many pieces of the puzzle through his Word to help me know specific things about the future so that I may share them with you. I have had two separate out of body experiences in which I was shown heaven and hell.

I'm a watchman – one of many in these last days – and a watchman's duty is to keep watch and warn the people as the final days approach leading up to the end. I know now that He chose me for this work because I am a warrior. I have fought throughout every step of my life against the evil that has constantly tried to thwart this work – my God given purpose. I seek justice and truth in every part of my life and most of all, I won't quit the task that is laid out before me – to reveal the fact that in this world, we ALL fight a spiritual battle! In Ephesians 6:12 it says, *For we are not fighting against flesh-and-blood enemies, but against evil rulers and authorities of the unseen world, against mighty powers in this dark world, and against evil spirits in the heavenly places.* You need to understand that there is a spiritual battle for your soul – where you will spend eternity – being fought between God and Satan! IT IS REAL, and I have witnessed it firsthand. Satan is a liar! In human history, he has deceived everyone with his lies. I am going to expose these lies to you so that you will be equipped to fight the good fight. I suggest that you open the Bible or any smart device – I have primarily used the New Living Translation or NLT and the King James Version or KJV where noted – and follow along with me as I reveal portions of scripture and what God's Word has to say to us. My book is a crash course about many topics found in the Bible. It is by no means a substitute for God's Holy Word. I pray you will read his Word and learn what God has to say to you!

Personally, I have read the entire Bible. It is my prayer that you will read the chapters of Matthew, Mark, Luke, and John – the gospels – and read the words written in red, which are the words of Jesus Christ. I pray that you choose to follow him now, and for the rest of your life. I must tell you, I grieve for the lost people in this world. The Bible tells us in Matthew 22:14, *"For many are called, but few are chosen."* God wants all to repent and call upon the name of his Son Jesus Christ. Sadly, most won't. There are 7.7 billion people on the earth today as of

2019. By contrast, the estimated number of Christians worldwide is 33 percent of that number or about 2.5 billion people. It has become my mission in life to share with you all the experiences that I have had with the Lord, the truths that I have been shown. I pray that no one will be lost. You are the only one who can decide where you will spend eternity. Choose Jesus and you choose life. Eternal life.

To those of you who have a relationship with Jesus, my book may shine new light on your study of God's Word. To those of you who do not yet have a relationship with Jesus – and particularly those of you born since 1981 – please understand the urgency of the subject matter. If you have not been raised in the Christian faith, you will be the group of people Satan will target and deceive through the coming one world leader known in the Bible as the antichrist. He will deceive you with lies and miraculous signs and wonders and prey on your unawareness.

I have included specific verses of scripture for you that are pertinent to these chapter topics. I pray that this book will open your eyes and that by God's grace, you allow him to reveal his Word of Truth to you.

CHAPTER ONE
THE BEGINNING
I WAS TAKEN UP TO HEAVEN

I was born in Lake Wales, Florida. My mother delivered me in 1961 in her seventh month of pregnancy. I weighed less than two pounds at birth. My lungs were so underdeveloped, I was in an incubator for the first few months of my life. I had to be fed through a tube inserted into my nose. I was so small that they sent me home in doll clothes. You need to understand…this was 1961! There was not medical technology like we have today, so the fact that I survived was a miracle according to my doctor. This was Satan's first attempt to end my life!

When I was 11, I was diagnosed with type 1 diabetes – Satan's second attempt to end my life. My doctor told me I would need to take three to five shots of insulin every day for the rest of my life. When I was 16, I saw an advertisement about juvenile diabetes. It stated that the average life span for a juvenile diabetic was only 26 years after the onset of the disease. This was very upsetting to me because I already knew I wanted to get married and have children one day.

At age 21, the most amazing miracle happened in my life. I was living with my stepfather Ben, when I had a life altering experience. One night I fell asleep as usual, and at some point, I was aware that I was no longer in my body. I found myself standing in the middle of the Roman Colosseum. I remember how large it was. I observed twelve older men dressed in sack cloth standing in a circle, and they were having a conversation among themselves. (I would learn later that these men were the twelve apostles.) All at once, they looked up into the night sky and pointed upward. I looked up, and I saw a man dressed in a purple robe with a golden sash, descending from the sky! He reached out his hand to me and said, "David, take my hand." I asked him who He was. He said, "I am Jesus." I reached out and grasped his hand, and we began to ascend into the night sky. As we continued to ascend into space, I was aware of how big the earth was! It was so beautiful. We stopped, and I asked him, "How did You make all of this?" He replied to me, "I simply spoke it into being!!!" He then put out his left hand and opened it. Out of the hole in the center of his palm (from his Crucifixion), bloomed the most beautiful red rose. It had many voices like an angelic choir singing praises to him, and its petals danced with the praise and worship music. I felt drawn to the music as it radiated throughout my soul and spirit. He closed his hand, and it disappeared. He said to me, "David, what I just did was no harder to do than to create this planet." He was pointing at Saturn, and I then became aware that we were indeed floating next to Saturn! It was so large and beautiful. I could see each of Saturn's rings and how they sparkled with something that resembled glitter. Looking around, I could see the vastness of the universe – all the stars, the sun, the moon, the planets, the galaxies – as far as my eyes could see. I was astonished! The demonstration of his power was mind blowing to say the least.

He told me the reason He had come to me was to let me know that all was well, and I didn't need to worry about being diabetic. He said I would live my life with diabetes. My life would NOT be an easy one, but He would take care of me. If I ever needed anything, just call out his name, and He would help me. He also told me I would live a long life and that I would get married and even have six children! I always wanted to have a family because I never knew my biological father. I was abandoned by him and that wounded me deeply. I wanted a true family, in the traditional sense, to love and care for and who would love and care for me. I felt in my soul and spirit that Jesus would never abandon me. He also told me that He had an important purpose for my life and that He would reveal secret and hidden truths to me during my life. The thing I remember most about Jesus was how loving and kind He was. I felt such love and peace radiating from him. He told me He loved me. The next thing I knew, I was back in my body, and I awoke.

~~~~~~

There are three heavens. The first heaven is our atmosphere. The second heaven is outer space. The third heaven is where God dwells. Jesus didn't show me the third heaven. In other words, I didn't see the "pearly gates" or God's throne. I look forward to one day being in the presence of the Lord in the third heaven with my family and all the saints who are saved by Jesus.

~~~~~~

I had always been an intuitive person, but now something was different. I was aware that I possessed a new ability to know things, almost like a sixth sense! I knew things that prior to this encounter with Jesus, I didn't. I could sense different things about people – strangers – just by looking at them. I somehow knew secret and personal things about their lives. I could sense that they were in either physical or psychological pain. This was one of the first gifts the Lord gave me, but it made me uncomfortable knowing these private things about them. I explained to my loved ones the things I felt regarding their lives, and I would tell them, "I don't know how I know what I know, BUT I DO!" I learned later in my life He had given me the gift of the Word of Knowledge. During my life, I was also given the gifts of Word of Wisdom, Faith, Prophecy, Tongues, and the Discernment of Spirits.

The very next day after my encounter with Jesus, I had a strong desire to open the Bible, and I began to read it. You need to understand that I was baptized as a Catholic when I was 8 years old at the request of my stepfather Ben. I had never studied the Bible up until this point in my life. I opened the Bible to Genesis Chapter 1 and started to read. In Chapter 1:1 it says, *In the beginning God created the heavens and the earth.* In Genesis 1:3 it says, *Then God said, "Let there be light," and there was light.* All of Genesis Chapter 1 regarding creation confirmed what Jesus told me when He said, "I simply spoke it into being." In Genesis 1:26 it says, *Then God said, "Let us make human beings in our image, to be like us. They will reign over the fish in the sea, the birds in the sky, the livestock, all the wild animals*

on the earth, and the small animals that scurry along the ground."

Now you need to understand that God is three beings. He is the Trinity, the Godhead. He is three in one – God the Father, God the Son, and God the Holy Spirit. To help you comprehend this, think about water. It comes in a liquid form. When heated, it becomes steam; and when frozen, it becomes ice. Water has three distinct characteristics, but indeed it is ONE in the same.

In Psalms 33:6 it says, *The Lord merely spoke, and the heavens were created. He breathed the word, and all the stars were born.* In verse 9 it says, *For when he spoke, the world began! It appeared at his command.* In Psalm 19:1 it says, *The heavens proclaim the glory of God. The skies display his craftsmanship.* You need to understand that I was just in heaven – with Jesus, and everything I had seen and what He told me was now confirmed in these verses in the Bible. I was astonished! At that point, I wanted even more to study the Bible. It was then I understood everything written in God's Word found in the Bible was true!

~~~✝~~~

In Acts 2:17 it says, *"In the last days," God says, "I will pour out my Spirit upon all people. Your sons and daughters will prophesy. Your young men will see visions, and your old men will dream dreams."* What had happened to me was now being confirmed by the Bible. And so, it all began.

CHAPTER TWO
STUDYING GOD'S WORD

So now there was an even greater desire in me to study the Bible, which includes sixty-six books. I was led to the books of Genesis, Isaiah, Jeremiah, Ezekiel, Daniel, Matthew, Mark, Luke, John, the books written by the apostle Paul such as the Book of Romans and twelve others, and the Book of Revelation. Little did I know, I was about start my education of the Bible – past, present, and future. One of the most influential Bible verses of my life is found in 2 Timothy 4:2 which says, *Preach the Word of God. Be prepared, whether the time is favorable or not. Patiently correct, rebuke, and encourage your people with good teaching.* This book will reflect this teaching.

I continued to read the book of Genesis. In Chapter 2:7 it says, *Then the Lord God formed the man from the dust of the ground.*

He breathed the breath of life into the man's nostrils, and the man became a living person. Now there is something I must explain to you. As is God, we are also triune beings made up of a body, a soul, and a spirit. Our body is our vessel. Our soul is our mind – our free will, it's who we are – our emotions and personality. Our spirit is the force that brings our bodies to life and gives us the ability to communicate with God through prayer, as He is Spirit.

In verse 15 it says, *The Lord God placed the man in the Garden of Eden to tend and watch over it.* In Genesis Chapter 2:16-17 it goes on to say, *But the Lord God warned him, "You may freely eat the fruit of every tree in the garden – 17 except the tree of the knowledge of good and evil. If you eat its fruit, you are sure to die."* In verses 19 through 22 it says, *So the Lord God formed from the ground all the wild animals and all the birds of the sky. He brought them to the man to see what he would call them, and the man chose a name for each one. 20 He gave names to all the livestock, all the birds of the sky, and all the wild animals. But still there was no helper just right for him. 21 So the Lord God caused the man to fall into a deep sleep. While the man slept, the Lord God took out one of the man's*

ribs and closed up the opening. 22 Then the Lord God made a woman from the rib, and He brought her to the man.

In Genesis 3:1-5 we see the serpent, the Devil, also known as Satan and Lucifer, speak to Eve. It says, *The serpent was the shrewdest of all the wild animals the Lord God had made. One day he asked the woman, "Did God really say you must not eat the fruit from any of the trees in the garden?" 2 "Of course we may eat fruit from the trees in the garden," the woman replied. 3 "It's only the fruit from the tree in the middle of the garden that we are not allowed to eat. God said, 'You must not eat it or even touch it; if you do, you will die.'" 4 "You won't die!" the serpent replied to the woman. 5 "God knows that your eyes will be opened as soon as you eat it, and you will be like God, knowing both good and evil."*

Eve believed the serpent's lie and ate the fruit of the tree forbidden by God, and she gave some to Adam to eat as well. In Genesis 3:8-14 it says, *When the cool evening breezes were blowing, the man and his wife heard the Lord God walking about in the garden. So they hid from the Lord God among the trees. 9 Then the Lord God called to the man, "Where are*

you?" 10 He replied, "I heard you walking in the garden, so I hid. I was afraid because I was naked." 11 "Who told you that you were naked?" the Lord God asked. "Have you eaten from the tree whose fruit I commanded you not to eat?" 12 The man replied, "It was the woman you gave me who gave me the fruit, and I ate it." 13 Then the Lord God asked the woman, "What have you done?" "The serpent deceived me," she replied. "That's why I ate it." 14 Then the Lord God said to the serpent, "Because you have done this, you are cursed more than all animals, domestic and wild. You will crawl on your belly, groveling in the dust as long as you live..."

<div align="center">~~~~~~</div>

Here we see the beginning of SIN in the world. It's very simple. When God says NOT to do something, we are to obey him. He is our sovereign God. He makes ALL the rules, and we as his children, must obey him! He knows what is best for every single one of us, and all would be well in our lives if we only obeyed him. God loved mankind so much that He made a promise to send a Savior, Jesus Christ, when He said to the serpent in verse 15, *"...And I will cause hostility between you and the woman, and between your offspring and her offspring. He will strike your head, and you will strike his heel."* We will find out later how God's promise came true when Jesus Christ crushed the head of Satan when He died on the Cross for the redemption of all mankind, and how Satan would strike his heel. Satan would indeed lie and trick many into NOT accepting Jesus Christ as their Savior, and he continues to this day. In verses 16-24, God punished Adam and Eve by cursing them and the whole earth and casting them out of the garden of Eden.

CHAPTER THREE
I WAS TAKEN DOWN TO HELL!

Just as Jesus promised, I was married in 1986. By the year 1999, I had four of the six children that He promised me – Jon, Jessica, Amber, and David – Autumn and Matthew would be born later. When I was 36, again one night, I fell asleep as usual. This time when I was taken out of my body, I found myself standing in HELL! I saw before me this huge area. It had a very high rocky ceiling. It was lit up with a very strange orange-red glow, and I felt the extreme heat that emanated from this place. My eyes were drawn to this lake of fire that looked like molten lava! In this lava, I saw many people, their bodies rising up and down like a cork bobber in rough waters. When they rose above the level of the lava, their flesh would melt away. This would happen over and over! The pain they were experiencing was so horrible, I had to look away. I will never forget the screams of these poor souls. Nothing could save them from their eternal torment! To say they were regretful they had ended up in this place was so tragic. Words cannot describe their remorse. They would call out for Jesus to save them, but it was too late! They had been given many opportunities in their lifetime to accept the gift of salvation from God by his Son Jesus Christ's death on the Cross, but time after time, they had rejected it. The pain and horror they were going through was too much for them – and me – to bear! I could smell the stench of sulfur and of burning flesh and death. I heard loud footsteps walking up behind me. They caused the ground below my feet to shake. I heard the most terrifying growl, and I felt something's breath on my neck and smelled the most horrible smell I'd ever smelled! I felt fear like I had never known in my lifetime, and I could not turn around to look at who or what was behind me. I cried out for Jesus to save me from this awful place! Instantly, He put me back in my body, and I woke up.

I was extremely shaken at what I had just experienced. I prayed to Jesus and asked him why I had been sent to hell. Immediately, He laid it on my heart that I was to share this with everyone I possibly could. Do you think I was allowed to meet Jesus and that He would have shown me His creation in heaven and then send me to hell for my own benefit? No, I was shown this to share with you and to warn the world! I pray that no one who reads this book will ever have to be sent to hell! This pain and torment will be forever. How long is forever? FOREVER! This does NOT have to be your fate. You and you alone have the power to stop it from happening. I pray that the Holy Spirit will open your eyes and ears. I FOUND OUT THAT JESUS AND HEAVEN EXIST, NOW I KNOW HELL EXISTS AS WELL!

By the grace of God, I was led to many verses in the Bible that confirmed what I'd seen! In Matthew 13:50 it says, *"...throwing the wicked into the fiery furnace, where there will be weeping and gnashing of teeth..."* In Matthew 7:13-14 it says, *"You can enter God's kingdom only through the narrow gate.* (JESUS CHRIST) *The highway to hell is broad and its gate is wide for the many who choose that way.* (SIN) 14 *But the gateway to life is very narrow and the road is difficult, and only a few ever find it..."*

Now you need to understand that God has appointed ALL mankind, that we are to die once - our physical death. In Hebrews 9:27 it says, *And just as each person is destined to die*

once and after that comes judgement, ... This is what is known as the first death. In Revelation 21:8 it says, *"But cowards, unbelievers, the corrupt, murderers, the immoral, those who practice witchcraft, idol worshippers, and all liars – their fate is in the fiery lake of burning sulfur. This is the second death."*

What I am about to say is key to understanding salvation. The only thing that God accepts in return for forgiveness of sin is blood. In the Old Testament, animals had to be sacrificed on an altar as a blood offering. God gave his Son to shed his blood, suffer, and die on the Cross once for all mankind. It is the only way we can be forgiven. It is a gift. We must acknowledge that Jesus' sacrifice on the Cross paid the price for our sins. His shed blood took place of ours. By receiving this gift, we are saying, yes, I believe Jesus suffered, died, and was buried. And yes, I believe after three days, God raised him from the dead. His resurrection signifies He defeated death and demonstrated his power as Lord. Jesus becomes our justification – think of justification as "just as if I hadn't sinned."

If a person has accepted God's gift of salvation – Jesus Christ as Savior – that person goes to heaven. If not, he or she must be sent to Hades (another name for hell) because without salvation, sin cannot be where God is. Sin must be separated from God. Once the end of time comes, the second death comes. This is The Great White Throne of Judgment which is referred to in Revelation 21:8. All sinners are to be thrown into the lake of fire (Gehenna) and separated from God for eternity. This is the punishment for ALL sinners who refuse to accept God's gift of forgiveness and eternal life through his Son Jesus' sacrifice on the Cross. The Bible is clear in Romans 3:23 which says, *For everyone has sinned; we all fall short of God's glorious standard.* Is there any hope for us? YES! In verse 24 it says, *Yet God, in his grace, freely makes us right in his sight. He did this through Christ Jesus when he freed us from the penalty for our sins.* In John 14:6 it says, *Jesus told him, "I am the way, the truth, and the life. No one can come to the Father except through me."*

God is a righteous God! Adam and Eve chose to sin in the garden of Eden by disobeying God's command. God placed the curse on the world and all mankind as part of the punishment for their disobedience. Now you need to understand what I am about to say. <u>Once you are conceived in your mother's womb, you are an eternal being. In other words, you will live forever</u>!

The choice is yours and yours alone, where you will spend eternity. God created heaven for himself and Jesus and the Holy Spirit and his Angels and those who put their trust in his Son Jesus Christ. Hell was created for Satan and his fallen angels, known as demons, who rebelled against God. I will explain.

Satan was created as the most beautiful angel of all. He was given great power. When Satan rebelled against God – because he was jealous of God and thought he could be God – he convinced one third of the angels to worship him and not God. God punished Satan and the rebellious angels and cast them out of the third heaven and gave Satan and the fallen angels the earth to rule and reign over. As I explained earlier, there are three heavens. The first heaven is our atmosphere. The second heaven is outer space. The third heaven is where God dwells. Satan is called the god of this world, and he rules it with his fallen angels known as demons. Satan was guilty of pride and wanting to follow his own will, not God's. This is how he tricks us in life. He is at work in our minds, prompting us to follow OUR OWN will, not God's. He does this by giving us the desire to do what we want for ourselves in this life, not what God wants. So, we are ALL being influenced by Satan to follow our own wants and desires, just as Satan wanted for himself. I believe that mankind is inherently good. However, because we are under the curse of sin and the influence of Satan, we often choose to follow his ways, rather than God's. This separates us from God. Following our own worldly desires (the flesh) brings death! Following God's will (the spirit) brings life! God knows what is best for us. His will is that we believe in his Son Jesus Christ. This is why God created hell…so Satan and his demons and all who choose to do their OWN WILL and not worship and follow God, will have their place of punishment for their disobedience to God for ALL eternity!

~~~~~~

In Isaiah 14:12-17, we read the story of the fall of Satan. *"How you are fallen from heaven, O shining star, son of the morning! You have been thrown down to the earth, you who destroyed the nations of the world. 13 For you said to yourself, 'I will ascend to heaven and set my throne above God's stars. I will preside on the mountain of the gods far away in the north. 14 I will climb to the highest heavens and be like the Most High.'* (Yahweh) *15 Instead, you will be brought down to the place of the dead, down to its lowest depths. 16 Everyone there will stare at you and ask, 'Can this be the one who shook the earth and made the kingdoms of the world tremble? 17 Is this the one who destroyed the world and made it into a wasteland? Is this the king who demolished the world's greatest cities and had no mercy on his prisoners?'* This refers to the Great Tribulation and the battle of Armageddon.

Because of sin, we too have rebelled against God. There are only two places where one can spend eternity – heaven…or hell! Hell is like the local jail. It is also called Hades in the Bible. It is where you are sent while you "wait for your court date," which is when you will go before God at the Great White Throne of Judgement at the end of time. The lake of fire is the penitentiary (Gehenna) – the sinner's final destination. Heaven is the reward for ALL who make God's Son Jesus Christ the Lord and savior of their lives! Do you want proof? In Philippians 3:20 it says, *But we are citizens of heaven, where the Lord Jesus Christ lives. And we are eagerly waiting for him to return as our savior.* In John 3:16 it says, *"For this is how God loved the world; He gave his one and only Son, so that **everyone** who believes in him will not perish but have eternal life."* In Romans 10:9 it says, *If you openly declare* (speak with your mouth) *that Jesus is Lord and believe in your heart that God raised him from the dead, you will be saved.* In Romans 10:13 it says, **For "Everyone who calls on the name of the Lord will be saved."** In Acts 4:12 it says, **There is salvation in**

no one else! *God has given no other name under heaven by which we must be saved."* In Hebrews 9:22 it says, *In fact, according to the law of Moses, nearly everything was purified with blood. For without the shedding of blood, there is no forgiveness.* And in verse 28 it says, *so also Christ was offered once for all time as a sacrifice to take away the sins of many people.* (He shed his blood on the Cross.) *He will come again, not to deal with our sins, but to bring salvation to all who are eagerly waiting for him.* In Galatians 1:8-9 it says, *Let God's curse fall on anyone, including us or even an angel from heaven, who preaches a different kind of Good News than the one we preached to you.* (This is the death, burial, and resurrection of the Lord Jesus Christ.) *9 I say again what we have said before: If anyone preaches any other Good News than the one you welcomed, let that person be cursed.* (DAMNED)

These are just a few of the ABSOLUTE PROMISES God has given us to prove that we are saved ONLY by Jesus Christ. Satan is the god of this world, and he has created the false world religions and all the false gods in human history. There are people all over the world who worship Satan through these false religions and they don't even know it! Some people openly worship Satan and have literally sold their soul to him for fortune and fame in this world! How sad! His only goal is to confuse mankind and trick them into worshiping him instead of the one true God (Yahweh). In later chapters of my book, I will explain much more about this great lie which Satan and his fallen angels (demons) are using to deceive as many people as they can! As I mentioned before, hell was created for Satan and his demons – and all who have sinned against God. <u>You were never meant to go to hell (Hades) and the lake of fire (Gehenna), but if you don't accept the gift of salvation and the forgiveness of your sins given to us by God, in his Son Jesus Christ, YOU WILL</u>! God will not let good and evil coexist in the same place for ALL ETERNITY! This is not hate speech. In fact, it is the greatest example of LOVE, EVER! NO ONE IS EXCLUDED! We are ALL invited to be included in God's plan of salvation. In 2 Peter 3:9 it says, *The Lord isn't really being slow about his promise, as some people think. No, he is being patient for your sake. He does not want anyone to be destroyed but wants everyone to repent.* In other words, God is delaying the Second Coming of his Son Jesus Christ because He loves us ALL and does not want ANYONE to perish! It has been over two thousand years since Jesus died on the Cross. Just imagine the billions of people who have lived during the past two thousand plus years who have accepted Jesus Christ as their Savior. The point I need to make clear is this, <u>time is running out</u>! None of us know the hour of our death or when Jesus will call us up to heaven during the Rapture of the Christian Church (known as the "snatching away" which will also be explained later). If you were to die today do you know where you would spend eternity?

I have a few questions for you to think about. Have you ever lied to someone in your lifetime? Have you ever used the Lord God's Name in vain? Have you ever stolen anything in your lifetime? Have you ever committed adultery? Jesus said adultery is looking at another with lust in your heart. Have you ever desired something your neighbor owns? If you are completely honest, you have replied yes to some, if not all these questions. In the Bible there is known as what are called the Ten Commandments. These are God's righteous laws. They were put in place to show us that we are ALL sinners. These sins that I just referenced are found in the Ten Commandments. So now that you realize that you have sinned against God, do you think when you go before God and are judged, that you should be sent to heaven or hell? Be honest with yourself. This is why God sent his son Jesus Christ into the world, so we wouldn't have to suffer for all eternity! It is my prayer that everyone who reads this book, comes to the conclusion that yes, you are a sinner (as we all are), and that you accept God's gift of salvation through his Son Jesus Christ.

CHAPTER FOUR
WORLD HISTORY IS FOUND IN THE BIBLE

When we study the Bible, we find written throughout its pages what are known as prophecies (messages received by a believer directly from God to share or warn mankind of an event yet to happen). In this chapter, I will list some of the biblical prophecies that have been made and when they came true.

In Genesis 3:15, God promised Adam and Eve (the beginning of mankind) a Savior – Jesus Christ. This came true with his birth. (In chapter nine, I will list many other prophecies regarding the birth and life and death of Jesus Christ.)

~~~ † ~~~

The Abrahamic covenant was made between God and his servant, Abram (later to be called Abraham), who was born in approximately the year 1996 BC. In Genesis 12:1-3 it says, *The Lord had said to Abram, "Leave your native country, your relatives, and your father's family, and go to the land that I will show you.* In verse 2 it says, *I will make you into a great nation.* (ISRAEL) *I will bless you and make you famous, and you will be a blessing to others.* (Abraham is known throughout the world, in the Jewish, Christian, and Muslim faiths.) In verse 3 it says, *I will bless those who bless you and curse those who treat you with contempt. All the families on earth will be blessed through you."* (This happens with the coming of our Savior Jesus Christ.) This was the beginning of the Jewish people. In verse 5, we see that Abram took his wife Sarai (later to be called Sarah), Lot (his nephew), and all the people they had acquired in Harran, and they all went forth into the land of Canaan. In Genesis 13:14-17 it says, *After Lot had gone, the Lord said to Abram, "Look as far as you can see in every direction – north and south, east and west. 15 I am giving all this land, as far as you can see, to you and your descendants as a **permanent** possession. 16 And I will give you so many descendants that, like the dust of the earth, they cannot be counted! 17 Go and* *walk through the land in every direction, for I am giving it to you."*

Now you need to understand that this prophecy has partially come true. If we could only count the billions of Jewish and Gentile people that have ever lived on the earth from Abraham's time (1996 BC), until the current year of 2019, and the billions of people who will yet be born during the one thousand year millennial reign of Jesus Christ (coming in the future), we see how this prophecy in verse 16 will be completely fulfilled.

God's promise to make the Jewish people a great nation came true on May 14, 1948 when Israel became a nation! The Bible even says in Isaiah 66:8, *Who has ever seen anything as strange as this? Who has ever heard of such a thing? Has a nation ever been born in a single day? Has a country ever come forth in a mere moment? But by the time Jerusalem's birth pains begin, her children will be born.* In 1967, Jerusalem became the capital of Israel, only nineteen years from the date of the country's beginning! This fulfilled prophecy is a FACT of world history. It happened just as God said it would thousands of years ago! In Isaiah 46:10 it says, *Only I can tell you the*

future before it even happens. Everything I plan will come to pass, for I do whatever I wish.

Babylon's kingdom will be permanently overthrown, as written by the prophet Isaiah. It is said that the book of Isaiah was possibly written in two periods (between 740 BC and 686 BC). In Isaiah 13:19 it says, *Babylon, the most glorious of kingdoms, the flower of Chaldean pride, will be devastated like Sodom and Gomorrah when God destroyed them.* This prophecy came true in world history in 539 BC, when Cyrus the Great destroyed the Babylonian kingdom.

Alexander the Great was born in 356 BC in the city of Pella, the old capital of Macedonia. The prophet Daniel lived in approximately 620-538 BC. He wrote in chapter 11:2-4, *"Now then, I will reveal the truth to you. Three more Persian kings will reign, to be succeeded by a fourth, far richer than the others. He will use his wealth to stir up everyone to fight against the kingdom of Greece. 3 Then a mighty king* (Alexander the Great) *will rise to power who will rule with great authority and accomplish everything he sets out to do. 4 But at the height of his power, his kingdom will be broken apart and divided into*

four parts. It will not be ruled by the king's descendants, nor will the kingdom hold the authority it once had. For his empire will be uprooted and given to others. Alexander died in 323 BC (at age 32). His kingdom DID NOT go to his heirs and was split up among his four generals! This was just as Daniel had prophesied.

God promised to scatter the Jewish people out of their land to many foreign lands. In Deuteronomy 28:64 (written by Moses) it says, *For the Lord will scatter you among all the nations from one end of the earth to the other. There you will worship foreign gods that neither you nor your ancestors have known, gods made of wood and stone!* In Ezekiel 36:19 (written approximately between 593 and 571 BC) it says, *I scattered them to many lands to punish them for the evil way they had lived.* God would also curse the land and make it barren in Israel so that it was a wasteland, and no one would be able to live in it. In 1867, Mark Twain wrote, "Israel, a desolate country whose soil is rich enough, but is given over wholly to weeds, a silent mournful expanse, a desolation, we never saw a human being on the whole route, hardly a tree or shrub anywhere. Even the olive tree and cactus, those fast friends of a worthless soil, had almost deserted the country!" In Ezekiel 6:8 it says, *But I*

will let a few of my people escape destruction, and they will be scattered among the nations of the world. The prophet Ezekiel was born in approximately 622 BC. He correctly predicted in advance that this world event would happen! 597 BC is said to be the beginning date of the Jewish diaspora. In 70 AD, Rome – under the leadership of Titus – destroyed the second temple, and the Jews were scattered all over the world. This is a FACT in world history.

God kept a small number of Jewish people that were left in the world out of Israel for almost 1900 years, only to bring them back to their promised land! In Ezekiel 37:1-3 it says, *The Lord took hold of me and I was carried away by the Spirit of the Lord to a valley filled with bones. 2 He led me all around among the bones that covered the valley floor. They were scattered everywhere across the ground and were completely dried out. 3 Then he asked me, "Son of man, can these bones become living people again?" "O Sovereign Lord," I replied, "you alone know the answer to that."* In verses 11-14 it says, *Then he said to me, "Son of man, these bones represent the people of Israel."* (Between 1941 and 1945, Adolf Hitler and his henchmen murdered an estimated six million European Jews. After this world event took place and after all the persecution of the Jewish people by the rest of nations of the world from 597 BC until May 14, 1948, there was indeed only a small remnant of Jews left in the world, and God did bring them back to Israel!) *They are saying, 'We have become old, dry bones – all hope is gone. Our nation is finished.' 12 Therefore, prophesy to them and say, 'This is what the Sovereign LORD says: O my people, I will open your graves of exile and cause you to rise again. Then I will bring you back to the land of Israel. 13 When this happens, O my people, you will know that I am the Lord. 14 I will put my Spirit in you, and you will live again and return home to your own land. Then you will know that I, the Lord, have spoken, and I have done what I said. Yes, the Lord has spoken!'"* In 1917, the United Kingdom became the first world power to endorse the establishment in Palestine of a "national home for the Jewish people with the Balfour Declaration." As I have shown you before, Israel became a nation on May 14, 1948.

God promised the Jewish people their land would be revived. In Isaiah 35:1-2 it says, *Even the wilderness and desert will be glad in those days. The wasteland will rejoice and blossom with spring crocuses. 2 Yes, there will be an abundance of flowers and singing and joy! The deserts will become as green as the*

mountains of Lebanon, as lovely as Mount Carmel or the plain of Sharon. There the Lord will display his glory, the splendor of our God. Soon after Israel became a nation, they discovered many underground sources of water. This abundance of water has now turned a wasteland into farmland! Israel is one of the top producers of fruits and vegetables and flowers in the region.

God's promise that Israel would be rebuilt. In Isaiah 61:4, it says, *They will rebuild the ancient ruins, repairing cities destroyed long ago. They will revive them, though they have been deserted for many generations.* It is a fact that Jerusalem has indeed been revived and is the largest city in Israel! Haifa and Tel Aviv are the second and third largest cities in modern day Israel. Now to my point. The Jewish people were given the land of Israel when God promised it to Abraham. In 70 AD, the Jews were expelled out of their country by the Romans. They were in exile for almost 1900 years only to be brought back by God to reclaim their land! They are NOT occupiers of the land of Israel. IT IS THEIR LAND, AND IT WILL BE THEIR LAND FOREVER!

The prophecy in Nahum 2:4 (written in approximately 612 BC) accurately describes the invention and use of automobiles. It says, *The chariots race recklessly along the streets and rush wildly through the squares. They flash like firelight and move as swiftly as lightning.*

Daniel 12:4 says, *But you, Daniel, keep this prophecy a secret; seal up the book until the time of the end, when many will rush here and there, and knowledge will increase.* This refers to people traveling all over the world in airplanes, it refers to education, and it refers to the use of the internet and computers which have increased knowledge. According to IBM, knowledge is doubling every thirteen months! I believe you would agree that all this technology and rapid increase of knowledge is now a FACT in our lives today.

~~~†~~~

In Isaiah 17:1 it says, *This message came to me concerning Damascus: "Look, the city of Damascus will disappear! It will become a heap of ruins."* This prophecy was written by the prophet Isaiah who lived approximately 700 years before Jesus

Christ was born, thus over 2,700 years before it happened! Most of Damascus today is a ruinous heap! It is worth noting that in the near future, Damascus will be completely destroyed.

The verses that predicted all these events are FACT! Thus, this proves the absolute accuracy of the Bible. There are thousands of prophecies in both the old and new testament of the Bible. The fact that many have already come true, proves the existence of Yahweh (God). The mathematical chance of even one of these prophecies coming true is astronomical! Much less, the thousands that already have and still others that I will reveal to you later that are yet to come true. You might be asking yourself, how in the world is this possible? Everything is possible with God!!!

CHAPTER FIVE
THE SCIENCE OF GOD

The Lord has revealed to me many secrets of his creation which I refer to as the Science of God. As I have already shown you in Genesis 1, everything Jesus showed me in heaven (the sun, the moon, the stars, planets, and galaxies), is a fact of life, and we witness these truths on a daily basis. In Isaiah 40:22 it says, *God sits above the circle of the earth. The people below seem like grasshoppers to him! He spreads out the heavens like a curtain and makes his tent from them.* Pythagoras, who first proposed in approximately 500 BC that the earth was round, said, "If the moon is round, the earth must also be round." In approximately 350 BC, the great Aristotle declared that the earth was a sphere. Of course, we now know that the earth is indeed round. Isaiah was born in the eighth century BC. Yet, he wrote about how God sits on the circle of the earth, more than two thousand years before it was scientifically discovered to be round! And in Job 26:7 it says, *God stretches the northern sky over empty space and hangs the earth on nothing.* In fact, the earth is held in its place by an invisible force known as gravity and sits on a particular axis that changes to allow for the four seasons. In Job 28:25 it says, *He decided how hard the winds should blow and how much rain should fall.* Approximately 300 years ago, air was scientifically proven to have weight. The relative weights of water and air are essential for the world's functioning hydrologic cycle to sustain life on earth. My next point. We cannot visibly see air, but we can feel it. We cannot see microwaves or radio waves with the naked eye but, common sense and science has proven they exist! Again, I say to you, this is proof of a living God.

In Isaiah 13:10 it says, *The heavens will be black above them; the stars will give no light. The sun will be dark when it rises, and the moon will provide no light.* This is a reference to Matthew 24:29 which says, *"Immediately after the anguish of those days* (the Great Tribulation), *the sun will be darkened, the moon will give no light, the stars will fall from the sky, and the powers in the heavens will be shaken."* These two prophecies are about the Great Tribulation and the coming Battle of Armageddon which are going to happen in the near future.

~~~†~~~

Next, 2 Peter 3:10 says, *But the day of the Lord will come as unexpectedly as a thief. Then the heavens will pass away with a terrible noise, and the very elements themselves will disappear in fire, and the earth and everything on it will be found to deserve judgement.* How do you explain the fact that in 2 Peter, he used the word elements? Elements such as gold, silver, and other metals have been known about since antiquity. There are 118 known chemical elements found on the periodic table that cannot be chemically interconverted into simpler substances and are the primary constituents of matter, distinguished by their atomic number, i.e. the number of protons in the nuclei of its atoms. Yet elements were not scientifically discovered until 1669 when Hennig Brand discovered phosphorous, and he became the first known discoverer of an element! This Bible verse was written more than a thousand years prior to their scientific discovery! The Bible also accurately describes the atom bomb and the total annihilation from the effects of a nuclear explosion! In Revelation 9:18 it says, *One-third of all the people on earth were killed by these three plagues – by the fire and smoke and burning sulfur that came from the mouths of the horses.* (The horses are a metaphor of nuclear missiles from submarines and mobile missile launchers.) Also, in

Revelation 6:14 it says, *The sky was rolled up like a scroll, and all of the mountains and islands were moved from their places.* On the cover of this book, there is a photo that shows the sky rolled up in a circle (a scroll), moving out from the center of the nuclear blast! Once again, the Bible foretells the future over eighteen hundred years before the nuclear bomb was even invented!

How do you explain that trees and grass and other plant forms produce oxygen, which is what we breathe to live, while plants have been proven to absorb carbon dioxide, produced by our respiration, which is a substance they need to survive? This did NOT happen by chance – or in evolution, as the "smart guys" (scientists) of the world would like you to believe, but rather, this is an example of a design. To have a design, you must have a designer! He is God!

Look at the human body and how complex it is. There are eleven major organ systems in the human body. Each has its own independent function. In Leviticus 17:11 it says, *for the life of the body is in its blood. I have given you the blood on the altar to purify you, making you right with the Lord. It is the*

blood, given in exchange for a life, that makes purification possible. Scientists now know that life is found in the blood! It carries oxygen to, and carbon dioxide from, the tissues of the body, as well as the nutrients the body needs to survive. Scientists have also discovered that the tears we cry have a different chemical compound and shape, depending on our mood while we are crying.

And what about all the animals? Each is so different and so complex! I challenge you to go online and look up information about the Darkling beetles, found living in Alaska. This species of beetle can survive temperatures of minus 76 degrees! This beetle produces a sugar-based antifreeze, called Xylomannan, made up of a polymer of alternating xylose and mannose sugars. The beetle freezes over the winter and in the spring, it miraculously comes back to life. Do you really believe that this complex process just evolved over time? Come on, really??? If you STUDY science and nature, you will come to the conclusion that ALL of nature is intelligent design by God!

The Lord has left his fingerprints in all of nature. Again, I challenge you to go online and look up pictures of donkeys.

Jesus rode into Jerusalem on a donkey, and ever since that day, donkeys have a cross on their back and shoulders. Found in Mark 11:2 it says, *"Go into that village over there,"* he told them. *"As soon as you enter it, you will see a young donkey tied there that no one has ever ridden. Untie it and bring it here."* This cross on the donkey's back was a foreshadowing of how Jesus would be crucified on the Cross and a remembrance of how He died for ALL mankind! Another example of Jesus dying on the Cross is found on the skeleton of the sail catfish. Go ahead, go online and look at the pictures. You will clearly see Jesus stretched out on the Cross! You can see his hands, feet and body, and even the crown of thorns on his head. Still another example is found in a sand dollar. If you open it up, you will find five doves inside. In Matthew 3:16 it says, *After his baptism, as Jesus came up out of the water, the heavens were opened and he saw the Spirit of God descending like a dove and settling on him.* The Bible tells us how Jesus holds everything together, in its place and in its order. In Colossians 1:17 it says, *He existed before anything else, and he holds all creation together.* I challenge you to go online and look up the word **LAMININ** and the pictures associated with it. Laminins are high-molecular weight proteins and the glue that holds ALL the cells in our body together. And its shape??? It is shaped exactly like the Cross that Jesus died on!!! I wonder how scientists will explain this fact away? I am sure they will try!

~~~†~~~

Do you really believe all of this evolved over millions of years as scientists believe? Scientists work by the premise of theory, which is supposition or conjecture – an educated guess! I rely on the Word of God, and so far, I have found it to be fact – not a theory! Facts are stubborn things! Again, I say to you, to have a design, you must first have a designer. I will make this really simple. If you gathered some steel, some glass, some rubber, plastic, and electrical wire, and put these materials on your driveway, how many millions of years would you have to wait for it to evolve into a car? Well??? This is my point exactly! If you take these same parts of a car, and the people who work at the automobile factory who assemble them, then you will have a car! It had to be designed first and then assembled. This again is solid proof of God's existence. In Hebrews 3:4 it says, *For every house has a builder, but the one who built everything is God.* To have a creation, you must have a creator!

My last point. There is a famous artifact known as the Shroud of Turin. It is a burial cloth, said to have the image of Jesus Christ imprinted on it. This cloth is an image of a man with the markings from being whipped on his back and shows the marks of crucifixion on his hands and feet and side. Look it up. The

Gospels of Matthew, Mark, Luke, and John reported that Joseph of Arimathea wrapped the body of Jesus in a cloth before He was put into the burial tomb. Scientific tests have proven that the image is imbedded into the cloth by what is believed to be formed by radiation methods beyond the current understanding of science. It also contains human blood imbedded in the cloth. The blood type is AB and is considered VERY RARE! There have been carbon dating tests preformed on the cloth, but fibers that were tested were believed to have been the replacement cloth used to repair the Shroud that was damaged by a fire in the middle ages. Upon further testing of the section of the cloth not damaged by the fire it was discovered the cloth contained dust and pollen that could ONLY HAVE COME FROM THE HOLY LAND! Again, I believe that this artifact is just more proof to mankind of the existence of the Lord Jesus. He has left ALL this evidence about his creation and his life and death in plain sight, if we only look for it. Later, I will disclose even more evidence and more prophecies yet to come true that I believe you will witness in your lifetime.

CHAPTER SIX
THE ATTACKS FROM SATAN AND THE MIRACLES OF MY LIFE

I have experienced many attacks from Satan, but God has also done many miracles in my life. As I have mentioned previously, the first was when I was born in 1961. My mother was only seven months pregnant, and the doctors kept me alive in an incubator. What I'm about to tell you is real. These things happened to me over and over again in my life. Looking back over my life, I see how many times Satan has tried to end it, BUT GOD had other plans for me! The second time Satan tried to end my life was when I was 11. I was diagnosed with type 1 diabetes. Back in the 70's, diabetics were expected to live an average life span of only 26 years. Well, I am 57 years old at the time of my writing this book. The doctors treating me now have told me I shouldn't be alive!

~~~ ~~~

You've already read about the miracle – when I was 21 and Jesus took me up to heaven.

~~~ † ~~~

When I was 22, a couple friends of mine and I went fishing on Lake Toho in Florida. We rented a very small jon boat and set off to catch some bass. While we were fishing the weather changed, and we found ourselves in a terrible thunder storm. The waves were four to five feet high! They battered our small boat, filling it with water. We used a bait bucket to bail out the boat, as the storm began to subside. Little did we know, the waves lifted the motor off the jon boat, and it was now on the bottom of the lake! All the food I had packed was washed overboard. So now I was facing the fact that I had no food to combat any insulin reaction that might happen and no motor to get us back to the marina. Most of the other fisherman had left the water. Lake Toho is about twenty miles long and about four miles wide. I was so afraid that my blood sugar would drop from the stress and the effort of having to bail the water from the boat. We didn't have cell phones then. I felt hopeless! I prayed to Jesus to help us. Then I spotted the very last boat on the water. Thankfully, there was still an oar left in our boat and

I began to wave it in the air. The boater saw it and came to our rescue! He towed us back to the marina, and we were safe.

In 1988, I had a dream that my stepfather Ben would die soon. In the dream, it was night time, and I was just pulling into the driveway where Ben lived. I saw the roof of the RV he lived in open up! Ben was being lifted up in his favorite recliner through a tunnel of white light. He waved to me and said it was his time to go to heaven! Three months later, he passed away. He was found on the floor next to his favorite chair, kneeling in a praying position.

I was married in 1986. In 1989, we had our second daughter, Amber. She was only an infant when one night while I slept, I had a severe low blood sugar reaction. My wife was in the living room feeding Amber when she heard a banging noise coming from our bedroom. She heard a voice in her head say, go check on David! When she did, I was in convulsions and foaming at the mouth. The headboard was banging very loudly against the wall. My wife knew when she found me that I was having an insulin reaction. She called the paramedics, and when they arrived and checked my blood sugar, it was 17! Normal blood sugar ranges from 80-120. They gave me a dose of D-50 (a sugar mixture to inject into my vein) and rushed me to the hospital. I regained consciousness hours later and stayed in the hospital for 24 hours. The doctor said I almost died. Having blood sugar this low is life threating. Satan tried again to end my life, BUT GOD had other plans!

About a year later, I was driving home from work and had another low blood sugar attack. As I was driving down a back road, I began to weave in and out of my lane. A man who saw me driving erratically, turned around and followed me. I came to a stop sign and somehow stopped. I had blacked out and was unconscious. This good Samaritan pulled up behind me and got out of his car. He reached through my open window and shut off the car. He called 911, and the paramedics rushed me to the hospital again. When I woke up, the man who saved me was there. He told me he saw me driving all over the road, and he heard a voice in his head say, he's diabetic! Now this is where this story gets crazy. The man was diabetic also, and at that time, I lived in Florida. I never drove with my window down because of the heat, but on this particular day in my life, I did. So I ask you, what are the chances a diabetic would see me driving, hear a voice in his head, turn around and follow me, and then reach in my OPEN car window and shut off my car? I say it wasn't chance at all! It was the hand of God! I was unconscious and somehow my car stopped at the stop sign, and the man was able to shut my car off! God has literally saved my life over and over.

In my late 20's, I was diagnosed with high blood pressure. There have been many times in my life when my blood pressure was over 200/120. In my early 30's, I was diagnosed with hypothyroidism. This condition makes you gain weight which is not healthy for someone with diabetes. In my early 40's, I was diagnosed with stage 1 chronic kidney disease. As of 2019, I am now in stage 3, and I have a GFR of only 35. (My kidney function is only working at 35% of normal.) Again, Satan was attempting to end my life and keep me so distracted from God's purpose for me, even trying to get me to blame God for all my woes. After all, it was Satan who was attacking me with my illnesses. It didn't work! I had such rock-solid faith in Jesus that NOTHING could stop me! Over the many years that I have been diabetic, I have had many diabetic insulin reactions. Mostly, they happened during my sleeping hours, and almost all of them required life-saving paramedic intervention.

~~~†~~~

In 1997, we moved into a new home I had built for my wife and family. It was at this time that I had the second out of body experience when Jesus sent me to hell, as I have previously stated.

~~~~~~

When I was in my late 40's, my family and I were traveling on vacation to see my wife's family in Georgia. A few hours into the trip, I started having severe stomach pain. It was so bad that I had to race to an emergency room. It turned out I was having a gall bladder attack. The doctor treated me with some medication to help with the pain and allow me to be able to get back to Florida and have an operation to remove my gall bladder. This was supposed to be an outpatient procedure. However, during the procedure, I stopped breathing from a reaction to the anesthesia, was intubated (they were able to start my breathing again), and they went on to finish the operation. When I awoke, the nurse informed me about what had happened. She said because of these complications, I would have to stay in the hospital for a few days. Now, this was supposed to be an outpatient procedure lasting two hours. Of course, this was Satan trying to end my life again! I told the doctor I wanted to go home. He advised me against this, but I insisted that he discharge me. When we got home, my wife was helping to get me out of the car, and I slipped and fell into a three-foot deep ditch next to the driveway. I landed flat on my stomach! The pain was unbearable. My wife thought we should go back to the hospital because I might have internal bleeding from the fall. I told her no. I felt at peace knowing God was going to heal me. He healed me from this surgery within ten days – when the doctor said it would take four weeks because of the diabetes. I didn't have any further complications. I chose to stand in faith and to trust in God that all would be well as Jesus had promised me when I was with him in heaven.

As I have shown you over and over, Satan has tried to destroy my life. He had already been after my health, and now he was coming after my relationships. The next thing I faced was losing my wife and family in divorce. Satan started the most aggressive attack I ever experienced up until this point in my life. As I began to share with my wife the hidden secrets that Jesus gave me, she doubted me. I only wanted to share my experiences with her and my children. When I told them what the Bible said about heaven and hell and what I had witnessed, she accused me of "scaring the hell out of my children," to which I responded, it's what I am supposed to do as a loving

God-fearing father. I knew the consequences of not accepting Jesus Christ as their Savior, so I guess you could say yes, by teaching them, I did literally scare the HELL out of them!

My wife told me that she wasn't happy with our marriage any longer, that she wasn't in love with me anymore, and she wanted a divorce. We had extremely differing opinions on how to raise our children. I held steadfast with the teachings of the Bible, whereas at that time of her life she had an entirely worldly view. She would not back me up when I would punish two of our daughters for disobeying us. If I were to take their cell phones away as punishment for something they had done wrong, my wife would give them back without my knowledge and shorten the time they were grounded for. My two daughters would confront my wife and say, you're always taking Dad's side. She would choose to listen to them, rather than me. Consequently, we were divorced in 2014. From that time on, I had a horrible relationship with my two daughters.

My family life was destroyed, but there was still a miracle in this story. When my youngest daughter turned seventeen, she started going to church and was baptized as a Christian in 2018!

Today, we have the most loving relationship with each other. My second daughter and I have also made peace and are so close to each other. They both realize now that I was only trying to be a good father, showing my deep love for them by living out what God's Word has to say about raising up godly children. I am very proud of each one of my six children and love each of them very, very much. I am thankful that they are all saved and that we will one day all be together in heaven.

A year or so after the divorce, I met my wife Carlene. We married in 2015. Our story started on a Christian dating site. We chatted through the app. We exchanged emails, then phone numbers. For our first date, I drove from Bradenton to Ocala to meet her in person. She was there to be with her stepfather who was in the hospital. When I met him, he was sitting up in the bed. We shook hands, and instantly I could feel in my spirit, he would pass soon. I told Carlene that he would die very soon and that she needed to ask him if he had made Jesus his Lord and Savior. She prayed with him and led him to the Lord. Sadly, thirty-six hours later, he passed away.

~~~†~~~

From the very beginning of this new relationship, Satan began a fierce attack on us. A couple of years before my divorce from my first wife, I found out I had heart disease. I had to undergo a heart catheterization. At that time, I had several arteries clogged 40 to 50 percent. Within six months of my marriage to Carlene, one afternoon I experienced severe shortness of breath. Carlene called the paramedics. They came and took me to the hospital. I had to undergo another heart cath. My doctor inserted two stents into the main front descending artery of my heart. Later that day when he came into my room, he explained to us that my artery was ninety percent blocked. He said I had what was known as the Widow Maker. (In other words, this condition kills most men who have it.) BUT GOD had other plans! Two days later, I was back at home and began having shortness of breath, chest pain, and a rapid heartbeat. I felt like my veins were burning up inside, and I thought I might be dying. Carlene immediately held me and began to pray over me. Within an hour, this episode ended. About a year later, I had to have another stent implanted into my heart. Months later, on a future visit to my cardiologist, they gave me a nuclear stress test. The results showed I had another heart blockage, and he needed to perform another heart cath. He showed me the picture, stating I had at least an eighty percent blockage. The heart catheterization was scheduled for about a week later. Before the procedure, Carlene and I prayed to Jesus and asked him to perform a miracle on my heart, not only for me, but also to reveal himself to the doctor and the medical staff who were in the operating room. In surgery, the doctor tried to find the new blockage, but it was not there! All my previous stents were healed! They were stunned! God answered our prayer. It was a miracle. Praise the Lord! They had all the scientific evidence to show there was a blockage in my artery, and now it was gone!

~~~~~~

A few months later, I woke up on a Thursday morning, and I was completely deaf! I woke Carlene up and told her what was happening. I started to cry because I couldn't hear my voice or hers. She began praying for me in the spirit. I felt a calm come over me and somehow, I knew I was going to be okay. Two days later, we went to a healing conference in Miami. The elders of the church were praying over people. When it was my turn, a young man prayed over me. After he laid his hands on me, I could slightly hear again! Seven more people prayed over me during the rest of the day, and when it was over, I could hear again! Praise Jesus!!!

~~~†~~~

Satan continued his relational attack on me by causing almost everything Carlene said to me to be misinterpreted. I would react with anger which caused us to argue week after week! Dealing with everything going on with my health and now in my newly married life, I would get so distraught that I would leave our home and move in with my oldest son who lived 50 miles away. This pattern repeated itself over the next two years. You need to understand that I was not only dealing with the loss of my first marriage and my children, but the fact that my seven-year old son was now living 450 miles away from me, and I didn't get to spend much time with him. It was too much to bear!

My new mother-in-law's health was failing, and we moved her in with us. I had a dream that she would wander away out of our house and get lost. This did happen to her mom as she suffered from Parkinson's disease and early signs of dementia. She also had congestive heart failure. One morning while Carlene was at work, I came home and found her mom, lost and confused, walking around our neighborhood.

~~~~~~

I felt in my spirit that her mom would soon pass. She was being treated by hospice for almost two years when ironically, her doctor told her that she wasn't sick enough to remain on hospice care. I strongly advised the doctor not to discharge her. She passed away five days after hospice discharged her from their care. This was just further confirmation of the gift God had given me. Since my visit with Jesus in heaven, I have known things that would happen before they did.

~~~~~~

Carlene and I continued to fight, and it got so bad that I filed for divorce. This is where the miracle began. Carlene confided in one of her coworkers about our situation, and she suggested that maybe we needed some time apart. I reluctantly agreed and moved out. During the next few months, the Lord showed me that because of all the past rejection and hurt that I went through in previous relationships, I had been overly sensitive toward Carlene. He had sent her – this godly woman – especially just for me to be my helpmeet, my wife, to help me with my calling and what lied ahead. After realizing I was wrong, I met with my wife and apologized to her, and we decided to postpone the divorce. Through much prayer, and prayer from dear friends, godly counsel, and eventually attending a couple's class sponsored by the University of Florida, we began to learn about and work through our challenges. We believe God is healing our hearts and our marriage. I moved back in, and I have never loved, nor trusted her more.

Recently, the Lord has revealed to us that Carlene has been given the gift of healing, also known as laying on of hands. There have been many people that that she has laid hands on and prayed for that received healing! As I travel, speaking at churches and public events, we will invite those in need of prayer and healing to come forward. Carlene and I will pray, and she will lay hands on those who are sick. In Mark 16:17-18 it says, *These miraculous signs will accompany those who believe: They will cast out demons in my name, and they will speak in new languages…18 They will be able to place their hands on the sick, and they will be healed.*

Recently, I went to see an eye doctor for a checkup. I hadn't had an eye exam for about four years. Because of diabetes, I had what is known as Diabetic Retinopathy. When the doctor examined my eyes, everything inside my eyes was normal!!! He asked me, "why are you here?" There was no evidence of diabetic damage at all. Now you need to understand I was diagnosed with this eye disease fifteen years prior to this visit. Many times, the tiny blood vessels inside my eyes would burst and fill my eyes up with blood, causing my vision to be compromised. They had given me many laser treatments to help ward off any future bleeding inside my eyes. Now they were healed! It was a miracle! Praise Jesus!!!

I was led by the Lord to these verses in 2 Corinthians 12:6-9 which says, *If I wanted to boast, I would be no fool in doing so, because I would be telling the truth. But I won't do it, because I don't want anyone to give me credit beyond what they can see in my life or hear in my message, 7 even though I have received such wonderful revelations from God. So to keep me from becoming proud, I was given a thorn in my flesh, a messenger from Satan to torment me and keep me from becoming proud. 8 Three different times I begged the Lord to take it away. 9 Each time he said, "My grace is all you need. My power works best in weakness." So now I am glad to boast about my weaknesses, so that the power of Christ can work through me.* More times than I can remember, I too asked Jesus to heal me of my afflictions that Satan was attacking me with. But I am comforted knowing that even the great apostle Paul suffered for the sake of Jesus and the gospel. Jesus truly uses the weak to lead the strong. His grace is enough for me!

My point in writing this chapter is to let you know that we are ALL under spiritual attack from Satan and his demons! Each of you are going through your own trials. Over and over, Satan has tried to stop me. BUT GOD has a different plan for my life. This is true for the WHOLE human race. In this life, we each have a role to play. Every person's role is different, and your role is suited just for you and only you! But you must have faith to please God. You must make a choice as to whose side will you be on – God's or Satan's?

Think about what I am about to say. In each of our lives, we know people who display certain characteristics. The Bible tells us the differences in these characteristics and how to recognize them. People who have accepted Jesus Christ display what is known as the Fruit of the Spirit. In Galatians 5:22-23 it says, *But the Holy Spirit produces this kind of fruit in our lives: love, joy, peace, patience, kindness, goodness, faithfulness, 23 gentleness, and self-control. There is no law against these things!* In the same chapter verses 19-21 it says, *When you*

follow the desires of your sinful nature, the results are very clear: sexual immorality, impurity, lustful pleasures (excessive indulgence in sensual pleasures), *20 idolatry, sorcery* (idolatry is extreme admiration, love, or reverence for something or someone more than God; sorcery – or witchcraft – comes from the Greek word pharmakeia, meaning use of drugs, worship of evil, casting of spells, etc.), *hostility, quarreling, jealousy, outbursts of anger, selfish ambition, dissension* (a disagreement leading to discord), *division* (as in factions or small organized groups within a larger one, as is witnessed in politics), *21 envy, drunkenness, wild parties, and other sins like these. Let me tell you again, as I have before, that anyone living that sort of life will not inherit the Kingdom of God.* In Matthew 25:41 it says, *"Then the King will turn to those on his **left** and say, 'Away with you, you cursed ones, into the eternal fire prepared for the devil and his demons.'"* The apostle Paul warns that if you live a life like this, you will NOT inherit the Kingdom of God! ALL these things mentioned are currently happening in the United States and all over the world! It is time to recognize what is going on! Whose side will you choose to be on? God's or Satan's? The right or the left? You and you alone have the choice to make. I pray that you chose the right, which is God. (Interestingly, the Bible tells us that Jesus rose from the dead and now sits at the right-hand side of the Father. This is no coincidence!) You will make a choice by your own free will. God gives free will to each one of us. If you choose to make no choice, you have still made a choice. Let me explain. By not choosing God, then by default, you have chosen Satan! God or Satan, good versus evil. There are no gray areas when it comes to the Almighty God. You are either for him or against him. Now you need to understand I am NOT judging you. Remember, I am a watchman and I am only warning you. I only speak the truth, and the truth will set you free. In John 8:31-32 it says, *Jesus said to the people who believed in him, "You are truly my disciples if you remain faithful to my teachings. 32 And you will know the truth, and the truth will set you free."* (Jesus Christ is the Truth, and He will set you free from the bondage of sin – free from Satan.) In John 14:6 it says, *Jesus told him, "I am the way, the truth, and the life. No one can come to the Father except through me."* And in John 13:35 it says, *Your love for one another will prove to the world that you are my disciples."* (A disciple is a follower of Jesus Christ.)

Now I say to you, we can ALL see the hate, division, racism, and violence and just how nasty people treat each other in our country and around the world daily, thus condemning themselves by their actions. Are these people who do these things showing love or hate for one another? I know that you can see who's on whose side! Just look at the two main political parties in America. One party stands for God's word (the Bible's principles). They believe in marriage between a man and a woman, which is ordained by God and found in the Bible. The other party believes in gay and lesbian marriage. One party is pro-life, which is also found in the Bible. The other party believes in abortion. We have laws in our country that protect the lives of unborn animals, but in states like New York, a child can be aborted up until the mother's due date! Where is the protection for the unborn child??? Since 1973, there have been well over 54 million abortions. One party believes in love, not hate, as we see in the violent protests of the other party. I could go on and on about how the latter party is being deceived by Satan! It's **NOT** their fault – they are spiritually blinded by Satan! They are being led, like sheep to the slaughter, to hell.

~~~~~~

This is why I am writing this book – to warn those being deceived to turn from these ways. Please hear my heart. If this is you, then you don't realize it, but you are being led by Satan who is the liar of ALL liars. He has blinded you to his ways. He hates God's children so much that he will do anything to cause a soul to be lost forever! I know I have offended some people by this statement. These are NOT my words but the WORD OF

GOD! Believing in same sex marriage and abortion and claiming to be a Christian is hypocritical. This is what I mean when I say that you are being deceived by Satan. Remember God hates the sin BUT LOVES THE SINNER! God has the answer for each of us. He is Jesus Christ. You can turn away from your sin! Simply admit that you are a sinner and ask Jesus to forgive you. <u>For the Bible says ALL who call on the Lord Jesus will be saved. This is what is known as the gospel. It means that you believe Jesus died on the Cross, He was buried, and God raised him from the dead on the third day. If you confess this with your mouth and believe it in your heart, you will be saved.</u> The Bible says you become a new creation. In 2 Corinthians 5:17 it says, *This means that anyone who belongs to Christ has become a new person. The old life is gone; a new life has begun!*

I have most certainly sinned in my life! In my younger days, I was a piece of work! Almost everything I did was sinful. My addiction was to sex. I thought that if a woman had sex with me, she must love me. This was how Satan deceived me. Satan uses many different addictions like sex, drugs, alcohol, and others to keep you locked up, so to speak, and keep your life a complete mess. But then I became saved! And now I have a relationship with Jesus Christ! He is my Lord and Savior. He knows me, and I know him. He delivered me from the bondage of my sexual addiction! Now my family and friends ask me, who are you? You are nothing like you used to be! My point is that we have ALL sinned against God. But God gave us a way to keep us out of hell – the horrible place that I have personally seen, smelled and felt. He sent Jesus to die on the Cross! ALL are welcome to accept this greatest expression of love from God. He gave his Son as a sacrifice to die on the Cross, so that our sinful lives could be saved. <u>The choice is yours and yours alone where you will spend eternity</u>.

As I have shown you, Satan has tried to end my life over and over. According to doctors, I shouldn't even be alive! But yet I am! Because God is in control, and He's not finished with me yet.

You will also experience many attacks from Satan in your lifetime! He hates ALL mankind. You are not alone, and you don't have to fight this battle by yourself. Call on Jesus, and He will answer you. Are you ready to accept the sacrifice that Jesus made for you?

CHAPTER SEVEN
THE WAR OF THE MIND

Ephesians 6:11 tells us we ALL fight many battles against Satan. It says, *Put on all of God's armor so that you will be able to stand firm against all strategies of the devil.* Satan is a liar! In fact, lies are his most used tactics. He will try to destroy your life if you let him. Satan loves to attack. He will try to attack your body with diseases, your relationships, but most of all, he will attack your mind! Sometimes I find myself thinking some of the worst things about the people who truly love me. For as long as I can remember, this has happened to me. Because of negative thoughts, I have argued with many people in my life. My mind would make up unreal thoughts about people trying to hurt me. Over and over, I would think things like, she doesn't love me, or he is lying to me, or she is trying to hurt me! It has truly been a struggle in my life.

~~~†~~~

Has this ever happened to you? It may be that you have had thoughts of your girlfriend or wife, or boyfriend or husband, cheating on you. Maybe it's not trusting what someone has said to you. Maybe you spend your day thinking how poor I am, and how will I pay my bills? You may envy your neighbor who seems to have a better life than you do. Have you ever thought that someone at work is out to get you fired and take your job? Do you have trouble making up your mind only to find out shortly after you have made your decision, you change your mind? The Lord has shown me that there are certain people Satan will target the most. He will put thoughts into your mind such as, you are not good enough, you are too fat, no one loves you, etc. He will tell you that you are a burden to others and you will never amount to anything. He robs you of your self-esteem. These are only a few of the ways Satan will attack your mind! Rebuke him and cast those thoughts out of your mind! Remember, even if everyone else in your life has failed you, Jesus WON'T! He loves you just as you are. He loves you so much that He died on the Cross, so you don't have to go to the place made for Satan and his demons. The truth is, if you were the only person on this earth, He would have given his life and died on the Cross just to save you! Who in this life has ever shown you that kind of unconditional love and acceptance? Call on the Name of Jesus, and He will answer. We serve a mighty God, and through him, nothing is impossible.

~~~~~~

Please pay close attention to what I am about to say. Throughout my years of studying God's word, He has shown me many verses that speak directly about Satan's attacks on the mind. In 1 Peter 5:8-9 it says, *Stay alert! Watch out for your great enemy, the devil. He prowls around like a roaring lion, looking for someone to devour. 9 Stand firm against him, and be strong in your faith. Remember that your family of believers all over the world is going through the same kind of suffering you are.* In 2 Timothy 2:26 it says, *Then they will come to their senses and escape from the devil's trap. For they have been held captive by him to do whatever he wants.* These verses speak about the attacks from Satan and how we need to control the thoughts we have. I have lost so much in my life because I have listened to his lies. There are many verses to help WIN the war of the mind. In 2 Corinthians 10:5 it says, *We destroy every proud obstacle that keeps people from knowing God. We capture their rebellious thoughts and teach them to obey Christ.* In Galatians 5:17 it says, *The sinful nature wants to do evil, which is just the opposite of what the Spirit wants. And the Spirit gives us desires that are the opposite of what the sinful nature desires. These two forces are constantly fighting each other, so you are not free to carry out your good intentions.* In Romans 8:6 it says, *So letting your sinful nature control your mind leads to death. But letting the Spirit control your mind leads to life and peace.* In Romans 12:2 it says, *Don't copy the behavior and customs of this world, but let God transform you into a new person by changing the way you think. Then you will learn to know God's will for you, which is good and pleasing and perfect.* Each day, Satan will bring you the fight of your mind – whether you are a Christian or not! It is part of the war! It is a battle, one of many. When Jesus died on the Cross, He ended the war with Satan. What this means is Satan can no longer harm your soul and spirit (your eternal being) once you are saved. But Satan will battle your mind to keep you from living an abundant life and living for Jesus! This is why you must fight the battle every day with the help of the Holy Spirit! You must recognize when Satan is putting these evil thoughts of hate, jealousy, lies – and the rest of the negative things you find yourself thinking – into your mind. Remember, Satan is the one who gives you negative thoughts. The thoughts of the Holy Spirt are always good. Living life as a Christian is not easy, as some would like you to believe. Just look at the hell Satan has put me through in mine. But I am strengthened by God's Holy Spirit, and with him, I can do anything! The Bible reassures us of this fact. In John 16:33 Jesus says, "*I have told you all this so that you may have peace in me. Here on earth you will have many trials and sorrows. But take heart, because I have overcome the world."* The closer you are to God the fiercer Satan's attack will be! He knows he can't steal a saved person's soul, but he can and WILL make your life hard.

~~~~~~

I pray that you decide to accept God's gift of salvation through his Son Jesus Christ. But, you must be prepared to fight many battles. Satan will try to destroy your relationships. He will try to strike you down with diseases. He will try to cause you to become addicted to many different harmful things – alcohol, sex, drugs, pornography, gambling, and other vices! He will try to cause depression and anxiety. You can ONLY win these battles by the power of the Holy Spirit. The following Bible verses will teach you how to overcome.

~~~~~~

In Ephesians 6:10-17 it says, *A final word: Be strong in the Lord and in his mighty power. 11 Put on all of God's armor so that you will be able to stand firm against all strategies of the devil. 12 For we are not fighting against flesh-and-blood enemies, but against evil rulers and authorities of the unseen world, against mighty powers in this dark world, and against evil spirits in the heavenly places. 13 Therefore, put on every piece of God's armor so you will be able to resist the enemy in the time of evil. Then after the battle you will still be standing firm. 14 Stand your ground, putting on the belt of truth and the body armor of God's righteousness. 15 For shoes, put on the peace that comes from the Good News so that you will be fully prepared. 16 In addition to all of these, hold up the shield of faith to stop the fiery arrows of the devil. 17 Put on salvation as your helmet, and take the sword of the Spirit, which is the word of God.*

Stand firm against Satan! Rebuke him and his demons in the Name of Jesus Christ, and they will obey and flee from you.

I'm asking you to open your Bible and read it. Go to the book of Romans and learn about your salvation – God's gift to you – if only you will receive it. Again, I urge you to take a stand against Satan's constant attack of your mind. You are so special to the Lord. He loves you! You are not alone in this world. The Lord knew you before you were born! You can and **will** find the strength, by reading God's Word and by the power of the Holy

Spirit. Do you want total control of your mind? Then take it back from Satan. NOW!

CHAPTER EIGHT
THE TRUTH ABOUT THE SUPERNATURAL

For as long as I can remember, I have had many experiences with the supernatural. Jesus brought me up to heaven and down to hell. He has also shown me the existence of the great deception of Satan. What I am about to say is KEY to understanding what is happening behind the scenes in the dark world of Satan and his demons. When Satan and his fallen angels, also known as the sons of God or watchers, were cast out of the third heaven, God gave Satan dominion over the earth, the first heaven (our atmosphere), and the second heaven (outer space). Over many thousands of years, Satan and his demons have made a conscious effort to deceive and torment all mankind. As I have told you before, Satan is the god of this world, and his demons serve him. Satan wants all mankind to worship him and his demons, so Satan has come up with this plan of confusion so that mankind will have a hard time knowing the truth from the **lie**! The Bible is the ONLY truth, and you can only know the truth if you read it. Satan knows most people do not know God's Word, nor will they read it, so he fills their minds with lies, his lies!

Satan's first lie, the existence of false gods also known as aliens or the watchers. The truth is they are demons!!! Throughout ancient history, there have been many myths and legends about false gods. One of the earliest stories about false gods was about the Anunnaki, also known as "those who from heaven came down to earth." They were believed to be the offspring of the god called An. He had an earth goddess called Ki. They were said to be extraterrestrial gods. The Sumerians lived in Mesopotamia in 4000 BC. Artifacts have been found that tell the story of this belief and the interaction with these so called star gods. In Genesis 6:2 it says, *The sons of God saw the beautiful women and took any they wanted as their wives.* In verse 4 it says, *In those days, and for some time after, giant Nephilites lived on the earth, for whenever the sons of God had intercourse with women, they gave birth to children who became the heroes and famous warriors of ancient times.* In Genesis 6:2, we see the sons of God come down to earth and present themselves as gods and take the earthly women as wives. They are not gods, but rather the fallen angels later to be called demons or the watchers, that were cast out of heaven with Satan. In verses 2 and 4, it clearly states that the fallen angels came down to earth and had intercourse with earthly women. Their offspring were known as the Nephilites, and they became the heroes and famous warriors of ancient times.

One such Nephilite was Goliath. His story is found in 1 Samuel 17:45-46. Another Nephilite was known as Cyclops found in Greek mythology. Many ancient civilizations have myths and legends about these giants. The Bible is clear that these giants were the offspring of the fallen angels and they became the heroes and famous warriors of ancient times!!! This same story of the fallen angels is found in the book of Enoch. This book is not found in the Bible, but it does have historical and theological interest. It states that the fallen angels came down to earth on Mount Hermon on the border of Lebanon and took human wives for themselves. They created these hybrid giants (Nephilites) to destroy God's creation. Some of these giants were over twelve feet tall! The largest giant skeleton ever found by archaeologists was over seventeen feet tall! They were blood thirsty beings who literally ate as many humans as they could.

~~~†~~~

This was part of Satan's plan to wipe out God's creation so that Jesus Christ our Savior would never be born! In the book of Enoch, it says 200 fallen angels (watchers) rebelled against God. They were cast out of heaven along with Satan, and they came to rest on Mount Hermon. These fallen angels taught early mankind many things, such as occult secrets, science and technology, medicine, agriculture, metallurgy, astrology, astronomy, and the use of cosmetics. They also taught mankind about war! This is part of the deception that Satan and the fallen angels from heaven used to deceive the Samarian people into believing in false gods. Mount Hermon is located on the 33rd parallel north in Lebanon. If you trace the 33rd parallel to the exact opposite side of the earth it directly points to the site of Roswell, New Mexico. Roswell is famous for an alleged alien spacecraft crash in 1947. Here we see a direct connection with the fallen angels and aliens! What are the chances??? It is because the fallen angels are demons who shapeshift into aliens!

~~~†~~~

Another example of these false gods were the gods of Egypt. The Ancient Egyptians had many gods like Amon, Anubis, Horus, Isis, and Osiris. They worshiped a snake god named

Apophis. These gods were not the true God known to the Hebrews of Israel as Yahweh, but rather Satan and his fallen angels or demons. The Egyptian magicians were able to perform miracles because they were demon possessed. Another false god was known as Baal. He was the god of the Canaanites and was worshiped for his power of fertility and for creating the rain and dew of the morning. Greek mythology came into existence in approximately 18th century BC and consists mainly of a body of diverse stories and legends about a variety of gods. Some of these stories were about the origin and nature of the world and the lives of deities, heroes, and mythological creatures. There are many statues of these false gods that remain in Greece today. Greece is filled with many artifacts and long abandoned structures that prove these so called star gods had human interaction and were thought to be real. Another civilization who worshiped these false gods was known as the Mayans who lived throughout Mexico and Central America. The Mayan people worshiped a snake god known as Kukulkan.

These examples are only a few of the many false gods found in ancient civilizations around the world that Satan and his demons impersonate to trick mankind into NOT believing in the one and only true God, Yahweh! They all have many things in common such as pyramids (a pyramid is the shape of the Seal of Satan), huge temples, advanced science and technology, knowledge and use of metallurgy, belief in magic and magicians, and the worship of a snake god! The Bible clearly states in Genesis 3 that the serpent (Satan) deceived Eve! All these pyramids and stone carved snake gods found at these different ancient civilizations represent Satan. He preyed on their ignorance and wanted mankind to worship him. These examples are part of the grand deception and master lie Satan and his demons are perpetrating on ALL mankind! In this chapter, I will expose many more tactics they use.

Many millions of people around the world have experienced some type of UFO activity. I myself have seen them twice in my lifetime. The first was in 1999 when I lived in Poinciana, Florida. I was coming home one morning. It was in the winter, and the sky was clear and blue. Out of the corner of my eye, I saw a white contrail streaking across the sky at an amazing speed. Because of its speed, I knew it was not an airplane! I lost sight of it as it went down below the tree line. As I turned around the corner of the road, I saw a huge bronze metallic disk hovering about 300 feet above the ground over an empty grass field. I pulled over and just stared at it! It was at least 200 feet wide. It was very shiny, as the sun's rays reflected off it. I was about to call my wife on the cell phone, so she could see it also. It was almost a half mile from our house, where she was at the time. As soon as I looked down to pick up my cell phone, the UFO vanished! It was as if it had read my mind! The next time I saw a UFO was in 2008 in Punta Gorda, Florida. We were building a new home, and I was outside with two of my children, David and Autumn and my electrician. I saw a shadow go over my yard, and I looked up. There above me was a silver disk-shaped craft about 25 feet in diameter passing by. It was about 200 feet up in the sky, moving to the southeast very slowly. I told everyone to look. After the first one passed, six more passed over us one by one heading in the same direction! As these spacecraft, traveled a mile or so from us they turned on their sides and split in half and shaped shifted and formed into a barbell-like object used at the gym! We were astounded!

The Lord showed me some verses in the Bible to help me understand what I had seen. In 2 Thessalonians 2:11 it says, *So God will cause them to be greatly deceived, and they will believe these lies.* In Revelation 16:13-14 it says, *And I saw three evil spirits* (demons) *that looked like frogs leap from the*

mouths of the dragon (Satan), *the beast* (the antichrist), *and the false prophet* (the one world religious leader). *14 They are demonic spirits who work miracles and go out to all the rulers of the world to gather them for the battle against the Lord on that great judgment day of God the Almighty.* (This is the Battle of Armageddon.) It was now I understood what we had seen in the sky. Go online and look up photos of UFOs and the grey aliens. The UFOs are bronze and silver in color, and the grey aliens look like frogs!!! All of the so called alien experts about UFOs and extraterrestrials need do is read the verses found in Revelation 16:13-14 and they would learn the **TRUTH** about these beings!!!

If you go online and look up the archaeological sites of Puma Punku and Tiwanaku in Bolivia, you will find cities that were built over a thousand years ago that display incredible advanced technology. The rock formations found there display laser like cuts in the granite stone that today, would be hard for us to duplicate! Now I must explain something. These UFOs are advanced spacecraft made from different kinds of materials such as known and unknown types of hybrid metals, fiber optics, and the use of antigravity propulsion. These UFO spacecraft, have been recovered at crash sites around the globe.

~~~ † ~~~

There has also been some type of biological entities recovered at these crash sites. The Lord has shown me that the fallen angels that were cast out of heaven with Satan had advanced knowledge of metallurgy and technology that allowed them to create these different types of spacecraft. This is one part of Satan's lie! The second part of this lie is that these biological entities (the grey frog like aliens) are demons! They take the form of these so called alien beings so that it would appear to mankind that they are real outer space entities.

~~~ † ~~~

There is an artifact known as the Roswell Rock. It is made of stone. It has a depiction of the moon, sun, and stars engraved on it, and it has magnetic properties. Under an electron microscope, the design is embedded in the rock by an unknown process. The Roswell Rock was found near Roswell, New Mexico in 2004. Roswell is the site of the alleged alien spacecraft crash in 1947. In 1996, a crop circle appeared in the south of England with the exact markings of the Roswell Rock on it. Crop circles and ice circles have been appearing worldwide for decades. They are supposed communications by alien civilizations. The sites like the pyramids in Egypt, the Mayan culture in Central America, and Stonehenge in England are just a few of the archaeological sites around the world that were put into place by Satan and his fallen angels. Some parts of these archaeological sites could have been built by humans. They were built to honor these star gods. No human civilization could have built ALL these amazing and complex sites. Many of the stones used to build these pyramids and other sites around the world weigh over four hundred tons! One such stone weighed twelve hundred tons! NO amount of raw human strength could move them! The aliens (demons) assisted in building them by using the Nephilites' brute strength and a form of levitation.

The three major pyramids found in Giza outside of Cairo are aligned with the constellation Orion. Along with the site called Teotihuacan, located in Mexico, it too is aligned with Orion. Another example of a culture that worshiped these so called star gods are the Hopi Indians located in Arizona. The structure of the three mesas mirrors the three stars of the Belt of Orion. Archaeologists have found cave paintings in Arizona on the rock formations of star gods or aliens.

~~~ † ~~~

There is a famous author who wrote a book about alleged ancient aliens. He has tried to convince mankind that they are real and that they come from outer space. He is wrong! These so called aliens are demons manifesting themselves as alien beings. These UFO spacecrafts have been filmed performing flying maneuvers that defy the law of physics! The technological feats displayed by these spacecrafts are just not possible.

~~~ † ~~~

There have been many movies like War of the Worlds, Star Trek, Star Wars, and Independence Day that allude to the existence of aliens. Again, I say to you, this is proof of this DEMONIC LIE that Satan is using to attempt to make people believe in UFOs and aliens. Satan is trying to condition the world to these things, so we will accept them when these aliens make official contact with mankind.

~~~ † ~~~

Many countries believe in the existence of aliens. MJ-12 was the code name of an American secret committee of scientists, military, and government officials that was formed in 1947 to study the possible existence of UFOs and extraterrestrial life. It has been reported that this secret group has crashed alien spacecraft and alien bodies in their possession. The United States and Russia worked together sharing information with each other. In 1995, the space shuttle Atlantis docked with the space station Mir. This was <u>not</u> meant, as was stated, for the Russians and Americans to share scientific discoveries between their countries, but rather for them to study the possible existence of UFOs. These countries KNOW that UFOs and aliens are real, and they will make contact with mankind soon! They have been lying to us for many years now! The part of this story that the world leaders have missed is these aliens are NOT from outer space, but they are DEMONS!

Just last year in 2018, President Trump announced the formation of a new branch of our military called the Space Force. They believe that alien contact is imminent. This is the deception of Satan on the entire world! As I have said earlier, millions of people worldwide have witnessed these so called UFO spacecraft and alien beings! To prove that these different supernatural creatures are part of Satan's plan, the Lord has shown me that THEY WILL ALL FLEE IN THE NAME OF JESUS CHRIST!!!

~~~✝~~~

There have been many eyewitnesses who have reported that during their encounter with these beings, when they called out to the Lord Jesus Christ, these beings immediately fled their presence. If you speak and say, "I rebuke you in the Name of Jesus Christ of Nazareth, and I command you to leave my presence and go back to where you have come," <u>all</u> these demonic beings (aliens) <u>will</u> obey your command because of the Name of Jesus. Why would aliens from outer space obey this command in the name of Jesus? Because they are demons! **I HAVE WITNESSED THESE SO CALLED UFOs! THEY ARE REAL – REAL DEMONS WHO HAVE CREATED THESE SPACECRAFT!**

~~~✝~~~

Many UFO abductees have reported that the aliens performed medical tests on them removing sperm and eggs. They have also reported biological hybrid beings that these aliens have genetically created! Does this sound familiar? The Bible clearly tell us that the fallen angels had intercourse with humans and created the Nephilites. They are creating these hybrid Nephilite beings to introduce them into our human population. They will be part of the plan Satan has devised when the armies of the world gather in the valley of Megiddo to fight against Jesus

Christ in the Great Tribulation. Remember what I showed you in Genesis 6:4? The Bible clearly states that the Nephilites were in the earth in those days and also…AFTER THAT! Satan's only purpose is to deceive as many unsuspecting people as he can because he knows without Jesus Christ you will be lost forever, and you will end up where he is ultimately headed – the Great Lake of Fire.

In 2008, the Vatican said publicly that the existence of aliens could be part of God's creation. I believe that the Vatican will announce the existence of extraterrestrials during the reign of the antichrist. The Bible tells us plainly that God created the heavens and earth, the planets and stars, and the galaxies. He made man in his image. He also made angels. There is <u>nothing</u> in the Bible that says He made aliens! This is the great deception spoken about in 2 Thessalonians 2:11. The Vatican has its own observatory on Mount Graham in Tucson, Arizona. The name of the binocular telescope is LUCIFER! I wonder why it's named that? It is a clue! Does the Vatican know something we don't? Satan uses the tactic known as "hidden in plain sight!" These supernatural examples are part of the grand illusion that Satan is using to trick as many humans as he can. In chapter eleven, I will explain how Satan will use these UFOs, aliens (demons), and Nephilites (giants) to gather the armies of the world to battle Jesus Christ when He returns.

The second lie from Satan is the existence of ghosts. We all probably know someone who has seen a ghost or who has had some type of supernatural experience.

When my mother was in her 50's, she woke up one night and saw her deceased mother standing at the foot of her bed. My mother reached out to touch her, and she vanished into thin air. When my mother was in intensive care after she had her heart attack, she saw and talked with her deceased mom and sister. They were standing in the corner of the room, according to my mother. They told her that it wasn't her time to die. My mother stayed in the hospital for three weeks and then was moved to a local rehab center. The day she was admitted to the rehab center, she told the nurse that she didn't need a new clean nightgown because she wouldn't be there long. That night around midnight, she passed away. The next day I was lying down, and I felt hands rubbing my back. I jumped up, and no one was there! My mother would always give me back rubs, so

I assumed it was my mother letting me know she was alright. It was not my mother, but rather a demon!

~~~ ~~~

Other experiences happened to two of my daughters, Jessica and Amber. On one occasion, Jessica had gotten up to use the bathroom and as she walked by my son David's bedroom, she saw a tall dark shadow in the form of a man, standing next to David's bed. It looked like some kind of black mist. She screamed and ran back to her room, and the figure disappeared.

~~~ ~~~

On another occasion, Amber saw her Papa George, who was deceased, standing in the middle of the open closet door in her room. He smiled at her and then disappeared. It was not Papa George, but a demon!

~~~ ~~~

Shortly after that, Jessica and Amber were in their room when a doll that was on the floor got up and started walking and talking on its own! They picked up the doll and slammed it on the floor and it broke. They realized that the doll had NO batteries in it.

~~~†~~~

When we moved to Rome, Georgia, we bought a five-acre piece of land and built a new home on it. After we moved in, many strange things began to happen. My son David and daughter Autumn were in their room upstairs when a box of crayons flew off the dresser and landed on the floor ten feet away!

~~~†~~~

My wife had laid down on the couch one day to take a nap. As she was laying on the couch, she saw a figure walk by the television, and its reflection was only visible on the dark television screen. She ran into the bedroom and told me what she had seen.

~~~†~~~

The next experience happened to me when I was working on the computer. I was making a web site that had a picture of people standing around the feet of Jesus while He was on the Cross. Each person had a particular sin written on their back (lust, murder, lying, etc.). After I finished working on this project, the screen turned black, and the word f--k came on the screen over and over. It was written in red, and there were at least one hundred of these words scrolling up and down my computer screen! My wife and children witnessed this for themselves! I would hear a deep growl coming from the corner where our computer room was. Each time I went to find out where the growl was coming from, it stopped.

On another occasion, I was in the living room watching television. Suddenly, I heard a loud noise come from the kitchen that sounded like dishes falling into the sink. I ran into the kitchen and when I looked in the sink, there were no dishes in it! Once again, my family and I were victims of this demonic activity.

As it turned out, living in the mountains of northwest Georgia was too cold for me because of my health. My doctor advised me to move back to Florida. It was at this point in my life that the Lord showed me the truth about these supernatural events. These so called ghosts are actually demons also known as familiar spirits in the Bible.

~~~ † ~~~

In Hebrews 9:27, the Bible tells us, *And just as each person is destined to die once and after that comes judgment.* Then we will go before the Lord and be shown everything we did in our life. It's like a movie review. If you have accepted Jesus as your Savior, you stay in heaven. The Bible tells us this in 2 Corinthians 5:8. It says, *Yes, we are fully confident, and we would rather be away from these earthly bodies, for then we will be at home with the Lord.* In John 14:1-3 it says, *"Don't let your hearts be troubled. Trust in God, and trust also in me. 2 There is more than enough room in my Father's home. If this were not so, would I have told you that I am going to prepare a place for you? 3 When everything is ready, I will come and get you, so that you will always be with me where I am."* In Philippians 3:20-21 it says, *But we are citizens of heaven, where the Lord Jesus Christ lives. And we are eagerly waiting for him to return as our Savior. 21 He will take our weak mortal bodies and change them into glorious bodies like his own, using the same power with which he will bring everything under his control.* This is heaven, where the believers in Jesus Christ go upon their death.

Here is a passage of scripture about hell. In Luke 16:19-26 it says, *Jesus said, "There was a certain rich man who was splendidly clothed in purple and fine linen and who lived each day in luxury. 20 At his gate lay a poor man named Lazarus who was covered with sores. 21 As Lazarus lay there longing for scraps from the rich man's table, the dogs would come and lick his open sores. 22 Finally, the poor man died and was carried by the angels to sit beside Abraham at the heavenly banquet. The rich man also died and was buried, 23 and he went to the place of the dead. There, in torment, he saw Abraham in the far distance with Lazarus at his side. 24 The rich man shouted, 'Father Abraham, have some pity! Send Lazarus over here to dip the tip of his finger in water and cool my tongue. I am in anguish in these flames.' 25 But Abraham said to him, 'Son, remember that during your lifetime you had everything you wanted, and Lazarus had nothing. So now he is here being comforted, and you are in anguish. 26 And besides, there is a great chasm separating us.* **No one can cross over to you from here, and no one can cross over to us from there.**'"

Let me explain. Before Jesus died on the Cross, all the dead went to either the comfort side of Hades for the righteous

(Abraham's side, also known as Paradise) or the torment side of Hades for the wicked (where the rich man was). God will not let good and evil souls and spirits coexist in the same place after death. Ever since Jesus has risen from the dead, the souls and spirits of all believers go up to heaven to be with him. And the sinners, the lost, go to the torment side – Hades (it can be compared to the local jail) until the Great White Throne Judgment, which takes place after the 1000-year reign of Jesus on the earth. After the sinner faces judgment by God, he or she is thrown into the lake of fire for all eternity (the penitentiary also known as Gehenna). In Matthew 25:41 it says, *"Then the king will turn to those on his **left** and say, 'Away with you, you cursed ones, into the eternal fire prepared for the devil and his demons.'"* In Matthew 25:46 it says, *"And they will go away into eternal punishment, but the righteous will go into eternal life."*

Now to my point. There are no such things as ghosts! When we die, we do not get to come back and visit earthly people and haunt them! In the verses above, it plainly states that if you are saved, you go to heaven to be with Jesus. If not, you go to Hades (hell). Just look at the modern world we live in and how many television shows are about ghosts. They are everywhere. If these so called ghost experts would only read their Bible, they would know the truth behind this phenomenon. This is part of the plan of Satan! He wants everyone to believe that all souls go to heaven. In Ephesians 2:1-2 it says, *Once you were dead because of your disobedience and your many sins. 2 You used to live in sin, just like the rest of the world, obeying the devil – the commander of the powers in the unseen world. He is the spirit at work in the hearts of those who refuse to obey God.* (This refers to those who sin.) As I have mentioned before, Satan initially resided in the third heaven. This is where Father God, Jesus, the Holy Spirit, God's angels, and those who are saved dwell. Satan betrayed God. God cast him and his angels out of the third heaven, and made him the god of the second heaven, and the first heaven. Then God gave the earth to Satan and his fallen angels to rule and reign over. Satan thought he could be a god, so now he has his kingdom here on earth. He is at work in every aspect of life – television and movies and radio waves! Thus, he is known as the ruler of the kingdom of the air or the prince of the power of the air. Ghosts are demons pretending to be your lost loved ones, and they want everyone to believe that ALL SOULS go to heaven. If you ever encounter one of these so called ghosts, cast it out of your presence in the Name of Jesus Christ and it will flee from you!

~~~✝~~~

The Bible is clear that NOT EVERYONE goes to heaven. Satan and his demons are the liars of all time! Remember what I showed you in Ephesians 6:11? Satan and his demons' only goal is to lie, trick and torment as many people in this life as they can into NOT making Jesus Christ their Savior because they know, without Christ, you will be lost forever!

~~~✝~~~

The next strategy from Satan is hidden demonic influence. Over many years now, the Lord has shown me the existence of demonic hidden messages in recordings of songs. The first one was "Stairway to Heaven," by the rock band Led Zeppelin. If you go online to YouTube and listen to that song played <u>backwards</u>, about halfway through the song you will hear, "So here's to my sweet Satan. The other's little path (a reference to Matthew 7:13-14) would make me sad, whose power is faith (Christians). He'll give those with him 666. (Satan will give them the mark of the beast through the False Prophet.) And all of the evil fools (sinners), they know he (Satan) made us suffer sadly." When you listen to the song in its original form, you hear, "If there's a bustle in your hedgerow, don't be alarmed now, it's just a spring clean for the may queen. Yes, there are two paths you can go by (Jesus or Satan), but in the long run, there's still time to change the road you're on." This is what I mean when I say, it's your choice, heaven or hell. Now I challenge you to go online and hear this for yourself. It is irrefutable proof of Satan and that evil exists! THIS is the all-time most played song on rock radio! Millions of people worldwide have heard it. What are the chances that this song with its demonic hidden message would be the all-time most played song on rock radio??? My next point. If you go back on YouTube and listen to the original recording of the Christian song "Amazing Grace" backwards starting at the beginning, you will hear, Mandy, Mandy, OH F--K....... These voices are demons, in shear agony, moaning and screaming over the lyrics of this song! Amazing Grace is the number one all-time most loved Christian song! What are the chances???

~~~~~~

To deceive the young people of the world, Satan has also used an artist named Ke$ha. She has a song called "Die Young." Look it up on YouTube. There are demonic graphics throughout the video. In the beginning, you will see a hearse with the word EVIL on it! You will see upside down Christian crosses and pyramids. You will see Satanic pentagrams. The entire video is about having premarital sex with many different partners, which is contrary to God's word! This young musical artist is promoting the kingdom of Satan. We can only pray for her eyes and ears to be opened through the Holy Spirit that she will come to her senses and repent and accept Jesus Christ as her Savior.

~~~~~~

The next proof of demonic activity is found on President Obama's "YES WE CAN!" campaign slogan. Go on YouTube and listen to it. When it is played <u>backwards</u>, it says, "thank you Satan!" When you listen to the thousands of people chanting, "YES WE CAN" over and over, then listen to it played <u>backwards</u>, it is so creepy! They are all chanting, "thank you Satan," and they don't even know it!

~~~~~~

When President Obama gave his acceptance speech at Invesco Field in Denver, Colorado in 2008, he was standing beneath the statue of the white horse. He said, "Let me express, let me express!" When this is played <u>backwards</u> it says, "serve Satan, serve Satan!" The Bible tells us in Revelation 6:2 that the antichrist comes to power riding a white horse!!! Now if you are one of those people who don't believe what you hear on those videos on the web, then go onto your own phone or computer, download the program called Audacity, and record yourself saying, "YES WE CAN." Then play it backwards. You will hear YOUR VOICE saying, "thank you Satan!" These are only a couple of many satanic dark sentences that Obama has spoken in many of his speeches! In the King James Version of the Bible, in Daniel 8:23 it states, *and in the latter time of their kingdom, when the transgressors are come to the full, a king of fierce countenance, and understanding dark sentences, shall stand up.* I believe this is proof that Barak Obama both understands and speaks in dark sentences!!!

Another clue the Lord revealed to me is found in Luke 10:18. Jesus says, *"Yes," he told them, "I saw Satan fall from heaven like lightning!"* Now you NEED to understand this! Go online and look up the Hebrew word for lightning in the Strong's Concordance #1300. The word is Baraq. Next look up the word for a high place #1116 (heavens). The word is Bamah! Lightning strikes down to the earth. Jesus saw Satan fall as lightning from heaven, thus Baraq Bamah! Could it be that Jesus was revealing to the world who the antichrist is? His 2008 campaign logo represents an image of the rising sun! In Isaiah 14:12 it says, *"How you are fallen from heaven, O shining star, son of the morning!* Which is the rising of the sun! What are the chances??? The term "Obama Nation" was coined during his presidency. In Matthew 24:15 of the King James Version of the

Bible it says, *When ye therefore shall see the abomination of desolation, spoken of by Daniel the prophet, stand in the holy place, (whoso readeth, let him understand:)* I believe Obama Nation sounds very much like the word abomination and predicts his reign as the antichrist! In 2009, President Obama won the Nobel Peace Prize. In my opinion, he did nothing to earn it! The Huffington Post produced an article with President Obama shown on a painting titled "The Truth" stretched out on a cross with a crown of thorns on his head. This painting was a mockery to our Lord Jesus Christ! While in office, the name of his government issued black Cadillac limousine was called the Beast, which is what the Bible calls the antichrist! When Obama went to Israel, they brought the Beast limousine with him to chauffer him around. While there the limousine would NOT START because the limo driver put regular gas in the tank instead of diesel fuel! God would not allow it to start! I believe the antichrist will be a Muslim. He is known as the Mahdi in the Islamic faith. Barack Hussein Obama is a Muslim! I urge you to go online and research the evidence I have presented. All these signs seem to point to Obama as the antichrist! Only time will tell. Whether he is or isn't, you will see the antichrist come to power very shortly, and he will be Muslim. You will recognize him by this. He will sign a seven-year peace treaty with Israel and many Arab countries and become the one world leader!!!

~~~†~~~

The next demonstration of demonic activity the Lord revealed to me is in the names, addresses, and logos of various international companies. Go online and look up information about Lucent Technologies. Their logo is a snake named Ouroboros that is chasing its tail in his mouth. Their New York office building address is 666 Fifth Avenue.

Google Chrome's logo is a circle with 666 embedded within its design. It is exactly the same design as the Divine King Sign 666. Google Play's logo is a pyramid shaped design that is exactly the shape of the Seal of Satan! Google GPS resembles the Eye of Providence. The company logo Walt Disney written in cursive has 666 embedded in it. A company called Lucius has 666 in its logo. Monster Energy has a logo that hails Satan. There are three lines that seem to make up the letter M. They are three Hebrew letters called Vavs that have a numerical value of 6. The number of man or 666!!! Nickelodeon has the eyes of Horus, pyramids, and the Zeus thunderbolt. Don't take my word for it. Go online and see ALL this evidence for yourself. Everything is hidden in plain sight! There is as much evidence of Satan in this world as there is of Yahweh our God!!!

~~~ † ~~~

The thing that I have tried to show you is that evil exists! Satan and his demons exist! Satan weaves all these lies to keep mankind so confused that people don't know what to believe! ALL of this is leading up to the end when the antichrist (the one world leader) will take control of the entire world. While this one world leader has power, these so called aliens and Nephilites will return to earth and make themselves known to mankind! I pray for each of you who have NOT accepted Jesus Christ as your Savior yet, that you do so now.

CHAPTER NINE
THE PROPHECIES OF JESUS CHRIST FOUND IN THE BIBLE

Since I have been in heaven and met Jesus personally, I don't have to believe He exists or hope He exists. I KNOW HE EXISTS! That is why I want to share my testimony with you, so you can believe in him as well. Throughout my study of the Bible for the past 35 years, God has shown me many verses about the birth, life, and death of His Son Jesus Christ.

In Genesis 3:15 it says, *"And I will cause hostility between you* (Satan) *and the woman* (Eve), *and between your offspring and her offspring. He will strike your head, and you will strike his heel."* This verse is a reference to the lineage of Jesus, going back to Adam. Another word for offspring is seed. Jesus was the seed of Eve, and the prophecy came true. The bruised heel refers to the crucifixion of Christ, and the bruised or crushed head refers to Christ overcoming death and defeating Satan on the Cross.

In Genesis 12:3 it says, *"I will bless those who bless you and curse those who treat you with contempt. All the families on earth will be blessed through you."* There were forty-one generations from Abraham to the birth of Jesus according to the book of Matthew and billions of families on earth have been blessed with the gift of salvation through Jesus Christ.

In Micah 5:2 it says, *But you, O Bethlehem Ephrathah, are only a small village among all the people of Judah. Yet a ruler of Israel, whose origins are in the distant past, will come from you on my behalf.* It is recorded in the Bible and in world history that Jesus was born in Bethlehem.

~~~†~~~

In Isaiah 7:14 it says, *All right then, the Lord himself will give you the sign. Look! The virgin will conceive a child! She will give birth to a son and will call him Immanuel (which means 'God is with us').* This is also a fact found in the Bible and recorded in world history about Jesus. His mother was the Virgin Mary.

~~~†~~~

In Hosea 11:1 it says, *"When Israel was a child, I loved him, and I called my son out of Egypt.* This is speaking about Jesus, when Joseph and Mary would flee Egypt.

~~~†~~~

In Matthew 2:23 it says, *So the family went and lived in a town called Nazareth. This fulfilled what the prophets had said: "He will be called a Nazarene."* He was known as Jesus the Nazarene.

~~~†~~~

In Psalm 22:16 it says, *My enemies surround me like a pack of dogs; an evil gang closes in on me. They have pierced my hands and feet.* Jesus was crucified at the site known as Golgotha.

~~~✝~~~

In Psalm 34:20 it says, *For the Lord protects the bones of the righteous; not one of them is broken!* In Psalm 22:18 it says, *They divide my garments among themselves and throw dice for my clothing.* It was recorded in the Bible and world history that Jesus received no broken bones from his crucifixion, and people cast lots for his clothing.

In Matthew 28:5-6 it says, *Then the angel spoke to the woman. "Don't be afraid!" he said. "I know you are looking for Jesus, who was crucified. 6 He isn't here! He is risen from the dead, just as he said would happen. Come, see where his body was lying."* This event was witnessed by many of his followers and the Roman guards who were assigned to watch over his tomb so that NO ONE could remove his body!

These Bible verses are indeed facts of his life and are recorded as part of world history!

~~~†~~~

The Bible gives many verses that prove Jesus is our Savior, and no one goes to heaven except through him! In Isaiah 43:11 it says, *I, yes I, am the Lord, and there is no other Savior.* In Exodus 6:6-7 it says, *"Therefore, say to the people of Israel: 'I am the Lord. I will free you from your oppression and will rescue you from your slavery in Egypt. I will redeem you with a powerful arm and great acts of judgment. 7 I will claim you as my own people, and I will be your God. Then you will know that I am the Lord your God who has freed you from your oppression in Egypt."* Psalm 3:8 says, *Victory comes from you, O Lord. May you bless your people.* (This refers to the Jewish people.) In Romans 1:16 it says, *For I am not ashamed of this Good News about Christ. It is the power of God at work,* **saving everyone who believes** – *the Jew first and also the Gentile.* In Isaiah 33:22 it says, *For the Lord is our judge, our lawgiver, and our king. He will care for us and save us.* In Romans 10:13 it says, *For* **"Everyone who calls on the name of the Lord will be saved."** In Acts 4:12 it says, **"There is salvation in no one else! God has given no other name** (Jesus Christ) **under heaven by which we must be saved."** In 1 Corinthians 12:3 it says, *So I want you to know that no one speaking by the Spirit of God will curse Jesus, and no one can say Jesus is Lord except by the Holy Spirit.*

~~~ ✝ ~~~

John 10:28-30 says, *"I give them eternal life, and they will never perish. No one can snatch them away from me, 29 for my Father has given them to me, and he is more powerful than anyone else. No one can snatch them from the Father's hand. 30 The Father and I are one."* And in John 5:13 it says, *I have written this to you who believe in the name of the Son of God, so that you may **know** you have eternal life.* All these verses prove beyond any doubt that Jesus Christ is the one and only Savior for all mankind.

There is a difference between salvation and good works. Salvation is the gift of God, but our good deeds (our works) earn us crowns of glory! In 1 Corinthians 3:15 it says, *But if the work is burned up, the builder will suffer great loss.* ***The builder will be saved, but like someone barely escaping through a wall of flames.*** So, once you have accepted Jesus Christ as your Savior, you can never lose your salvation. You can suffer loss of what are known as crowns. There is a system set up by God, whereby we can earn or lose crowns of glory.

~~~†~~~

The first is found in 2 Timothy 4:8 and is given to all who eagerly watch for Jesus Christ's return. It is the easiest crown we can all earn! It says, *And now the prize awaits me – the crown of righteousness, which the Lord, the righteous Judge, will give me on the day of his return. And the prize is not just for me but for* **all** *who eagerly look forward to his appearing.*

~~~†~~~

The second crown is found in 1 Corinthians 9:24-27 and is given to all who strive to keep bodily desires under control and to be temperate in all things. They know that by keeping their faith in the Lord, by running their race of faith after they have been saved, they will receive this Crown of Life. It says, *Don't you realize that in a race everyone runs, but only one person gets the prize? So run to win! 25 All athletes are disciplined in their training. They do it to win a prize that will fade away, but we do it for an eternal prize. 26 So I run with purpose in every step. I am not just shadowboxing. 27 I discipline my body like an athlete, training it to do what it should. Otherwise, I feel that after preaching to others I myself might be disqualified.*

~~~✝~~~

The third crown is found in 1 Peter 5:2-4; it is reserved for faithful ministers. It says, *Care for the flock that God has entrusted to you. Watch over it willingly, not grudgingly – not for what you will get out of it, but because you are eager to serve God. 3 Don't lord over the people assigned to your care, but lead them by your own good example. 4 And when the Great Shepherd appears, you will receive a crown of never-ending glory and honor.*

The fourth crown is found in 1 Thessalonians 2:19 and is for those who bring others to the Lord our Savior. It says, *After all, what gives us hope and joy, and what will be our proud reward and crown as we stand before our Lord Jesus when he returns? It is you!*

The fifth and final crown is found in James 1:12 which is given to those who have suffered for Jesus Christ and the Gospel. It says, *God blesses those who patiently endure testing and temptation. Afterward they will receive the crown of life that God has promised to those who love him.*

~~~☦~~~

These five crowns can be added to or subtracted from one's life based on how you live your life after you are saved. We earn these crowns during our faithful service to Jesus in our lifetime. We will lay them at his feet at the Bema Seat in heaven. I myself strive to gain all these crowns in my life of service to my Lord Jesus Christ because of what He did for me by dying on the Cross for my sins.

~~~☦~~~

I have tried to show you over and over, Jesus Christ is the only Savior that God has sent to keep us from the lake of fire. The choice of where you spend eternity is yours and yours alone. I have also given proof, beyond any reasonable doubt, that Jesus is real. He is our Savior, the only one who can save us from eternal torment. In Deuteronomy 30:19 it says, *"Today I have given you the choice between life and death, between blessings and curses. Now I call on heaven and earth to witness the choice you make. Oh, that you would choose life, so that you and your descendants might live."* (This is life, found in Jesus Christ.) Are you ready to make Jesus the Lord and Savior of your life?

CHAPTER TEN
LIFE IS ALL ABOUT LOVE

My dear brothers and sisters, in this chapter I will give you my perspective on the meaning of life based on what the Lord has shown me and how important love is to God. We were placed on this earth to love and serve Him first and then each other. There are over 500 verses in the Bible that speak about love. John 3:16-17 is the most well-known. It says, *"**For this is how God loved the world: he gave his one and only Son, so that everyone who believes in him will not perish but have eternal life.** 17 God sent his Son into the world not to judge the world, but to save the world through him."* God loved mankind so much that He sent Jesus his Son to die on the Cross so we wouldn't have to pay the price for our sins (this means spending eternity in the lake of fire, separated from God). In John 13:34-35 it says, *"So now I am giving you a new commandment: Love each other. Just as I have loved you, you should love each other.*

35 Your love for one another will prove to the world that you are my disciples." Now this doesn't only speak to loving your family and friends, but to all whom you have contact with. The homeless, the drug addict, the prostitute, the men and women in jail, the lady at the grocery store; the list goes on and on. In other words, all of mankind. These people need our love and compassion. God wants us to show love and compassion to ALL the least of these. Now the Bible tells us in 1 John 3:13-14, *So don't be surprised, dear brothers and sisters, if the world hates you.* (Jews and Christians) *14 If we love our brothers and sisters who are believers, it proves that we have passed from death to life. But a person who has no love is still dead.* In 1 John 4:20 it says, *If someone says, "I love God," but hates a fellow believer, that person is a liar; for if we don't love people we can see, how can we love God, whom we cannot see?* And in 1 John 4:16 it says, *We know how much God loves us, and we have put our trust in his love. God is love, and all who live in love live in God, and God lives in them.* One of the most important verses about love and peace is found in Romans 12:18 it says, *Do all that you can to live in peace with everyone.* It is up to you to show this love and peace to everyone you come in contact with.

~~~†~~~

For as long as I can remember, we have had a huge problem in our country with bullying. It has never been okay to bully someone. Just think about all the pain and hurt these people who are being bullied are going through. This is how Satan is at work in this world we are living in. He does the opposite of what God does! God is love and Satan is hate! Just look around you and all the hate that is in this world! As parents, we must teach our children not to hate, but to love each other. We must love each other as an example to our children.

We also must learn to forgive and teach our children to forgive. The Bible is clear that if we do not forgive someone who has wronged us, God will not forgive us when we wrong him. Jesus died on the Cross to forgive us for our sins, and all we have to do is forgive each other. This is love. To love is to forgive.

There are two commandments that sum up the law. Found in Mark 12:30-31, *"And you must love the Lord your God with all your heart, all your soul, all your mind, and all your strength. 31 The second is equally important: 'Love your neighbor as*

yourself.' No other commandment is greater than these." If you will just live your life following these two commandments, you are following the will of God. You see my friends, we must love one another, and we must pray for the people who hate us, just as it says in the Bible. By praying for them, we show love for them. If they verbally or physically attack us, we are to respond with kind loving words. It is impossible for them to keep attacking us if we are showing them love! When you show someone that you love and care for them, something in them changes. I have seen it first hand in my life over and over. Now by contrast, if you argue with someone, it will provoke their anger and usually leads to further escalation.

As I have pointed out before, we recognize, in this world these days, who have been saved by the Blood of Jesus by their character. They display love and compassion. The unsaved display the examples found in 2 Timothy 3:1-5. Therefore, we must pray for them and teach them what the Bible has to say about these things. The Bible gives us the very best example of how to love everyone. in Luke 6:31. It says, *Do to others as you would like them to do to you.* Now I ask you would you rather receive love or hate from someone?

~~~☦~~~

We have a horrible problem with racism, antisemitism, homophobia, and the list goes on and on. We are not black, white, red, or yellow. We are ALL children of God!!! We all bleed red blood. In the United Sates, other than the Native Americans, we are all immigrants. We are ALL people of color. My ancestors are from Portugal and the Scandinavian countries. Some of your ancestors may be from Ireland, England, Poland, Germany, Italy, or Israel. Our ancestors came freely to this country to have a chance to make a better life for their families and themselves. Africans were not given the same chance. They were brought to this country against their will to become slaves! This was wrong! They were treated horribly by our ancestors and are being treated unfairly today. Why are African Americans singled out just because of their skin color? This is wrong!!! We should look at a person's character before we assume the worst about the person or race of people. We must end racism in our country and our world. See the good in everyone! We must stop all this bitter hatred and division and learn how to love everyone. Please get to know your fellow men and women and see their character, not their skin color.

~~~†~~~

We have an epidemic in our lives today – addiction to electronic devices. Most everyone, including and especially children, are addicted to cell phones, video games, and social media. Most would rather be on these devices than to interact with people. Satan has succeeded in separating people, especially families, with these devices. When I was a child, we had no cell phones. We played outside together, we rode our bikes together, and we played in the dirt together. Today, your child's best friend is a cell phone or video game! This is another example of how Satan is trying to divide us, mostly the young people of the world. As parents, we need to limit the use of these devices and encourage our children to have meaningful one on one interaction with each other. Please limit your child's time on these devices and encourage them to have real relationships with people.

Please make a conscious decision to teach your children how to love one another. When you are out and about in your neighborhood, city or town, show love to all whom you come into contact with. When you love, you are displaying the love of Jesus. When they see you, let them see Jesus! Are you ready to love everyone?

CHAPTER ELEVEN
THIS IS THE END

In this chapter, I will give you a preview of the events that are going to happen in the near future. Throughout my life, the Lord has shown me what the Bible has to say about the last days. Soon, an event will happen known as the Rapture of the Christian Church (The Snatching Away).

In 1 Thessalonians 4:16-18 the apostle Paul writes, *For the Lord Himself will come down from heaven with a commanding shout, with the voice of the archangel, and with the trumpet call of God. First, the believers who have died will rise from their graves. 17 Then, together with them, we who are still alive and remain on the earth* (the believers in Jesus Christ) *will be caught up in the clouds to meet the Lord in the air. Then we will be with the Lord forever. 18 So encourage each other with these words.* Now I must point something out to you. If you go online and look at the King James Version of the Bible, in 1

Corinthians 15:51-52 it tells the same story as the verses in 1 Thessalonians 4:16-18. However, in verse 52 it says, *at the last trump: for the trumpet shall sound*. In verse 51, the apostle Paul clearly says *Behold, I shew you a mystery*. I believe that the mystery of the last trump is Donald Trump! For over a year now, I have discussed what has been revealed to me with my wife. I believe it is a sign from God that we have but a short time before the Rapture of the Christian Church takes place so that all can come to true repentance. Donald Trump can only be in office as our president until 2024. I believe the use of the words "at the last trump" predicted his term as the last president. When his term as president ends, I believe the Rapture will happen and God will call us home! When you combine all the other signs that I list in this chapter, I believe that the Rapture will happen very soon.

The Bible tells us what the world will be like just before the Rapture happens. In Matthew 24:3-14 it says, *Later, Jesus sat on the Mount of Olives. His disciples came to him privately and said, "Tell us, when will all this happen? What sign will signal your return and **the end of the world**?" 4 Jesus told them, "Don't let anyone mislead you, 5 for many will come in my name, claiming, 'I am the Messiah.'* (Charles Manson, Jim

Jones, David Koresh and others have claimed to be the Messiah.) *They will deceive many. 6 And you will hear of wars and threats of wars, but don't panic.* (Since 1948 when Israel became a nation, there have been many wars between different countries and kingdoms around the globe.) *Yes, these things must take place, but the end won't follow immediately. 7 Nation will go to war against nation, and kingdom against kingdom. There will be famines and earthquakes in many parts of the world.* (There have been many famines and both minor and major earthquakes worldwide in the past seventy years. Many hundreds of earthquakes occur daily worldwide, with major earthquakes of magnitude 7 or higher happening approximately once per month.) *8 But all this is only the first of the birth pains, with more to come. 9 Then you will be arrested, persecuted, and killed.* (Both Jews and Christians have been arrested, persecuted and killed in ever increasing numbers worldwide since 1941.) *You will be hated all over the world because you are my followers.* (There are many world countries that hate Israel and people of the Christian faith.) *10 And many will turn away from me and betray and hate each other.* (There has been a consistent decline of Christian followers worldwide since 1948. Betrayal and hatred are evident everywhere.) *11 And many false prophets will appear and will deceive many people. 12 Sin will be rampant everywhere, and the love of many will grow cold.* (These two signs are the most dramatic and evident in our world today. Sin is rampant worldwide and people everywhere only think of themselves.) *13 But the one who endures to the end will be saved. 14 And the Good News about the kingdom will be preached throughout the whole world* (during the Great Tribulation period), *so that all nations will hear it; and then the end will come.*

In Luke 21:25-26 it says, *And there will be strange signs in the sun, moon, and stars.* (We have had major increases in solar flares and solar eclipses over the past seventy years. There have been three tetrads or blood moons and many lunar eclipses since 1948. There have also been sixteen comets since 1948.) *And here on earth the nations will be in turmoil, perplexed by the roaring seas* (hurricanes and typhoons) *and strange tides* (tsunamis). (Since 1948, there have been some of the most destructive hurricanes, typhoons, and tsunamis in all of world history. In 2018, Hurricane Michael destroyed parts of the panhandle of Florida.) *26 People will be terrified at what they see coming upon the earth for the powers in the heavens will be shaken.*

~~~~~~

In Matthew 24:32-34 it says, *"Now learn a lesson from the fig tree. When its branches bud and its leaves begin to sprout, you know that summer is near.* (In the Bible, the fig tree is referred to as Israel.) *33 In the same way, when you see **all** these things, you can **know** his return is very near, right at the door. 34 I tell you the truth, this generation will not pass from the scene until **all these things** take place."* (This refers to the generation of the Israeli people born in 1948. In the Bible, a generation can span one hundred years.)

~~~~~~

In Matthew 24:37-39 it says, *"When the Son of Man returns, it will be like it was in Noah's day. 38 In those days before the flood, the people were enjoying banquets and parties and weddings right up to the time Noah entered his boat. 39 People didn't realize what was going to happen until the flood came and swept them all away. That is the way it will be when the Son of Man comes.* What was happening in the days of Noah? It was the same way as it now! Sin was rampant everywhere! The Nephilites were evil hybrids of the sons of God that lived on earth at that time. During the time of the reign of the antichrist, the Nephilites will return to earth and God will judge everyone not by a flood, but by fire.

~~~✝~~~

It says in 2 Timothy 3:1-5, *You should know this, Timothy, that in the last days there will be very difficult times.* (There are wars in the Middle East and Ukraine, civil unrest in Venezuela and Haiti, and division in the United states of America.) *2 For people will love only themselves and their money.* (This is happening worldwide.) *They will be boastful and proud, scoffing at God, disobedient to their parents, and ungrateful.* (All of these signs are evident in the world today.) *They will consider nothing sacred. 3 They will be unloving and unforgiving; they will slander others and have no self-control.* (Can you say fake news!) *They will be cruel and hate what is good.* (They will hate Jews and Christians.) *4 They will betray their friends, be reckless, be puffed up with pride, and love pleasure rather than God.* (People in the world are self-absorbed and desire earthly pleasures more than God.) *5 They will act religious, but they will reject the power that could make them godly, stay away from people like that!*

The key to understanding what Jesus said is, when you see **all** these things happening simultaneously, which they are now, then the end is near! Again, I say ALL these signs are happening in our world today. Jesus commented about the last generation (the generation that sees all these signs – they will not all pass away before He returns). If we look at the date Israel became a nation and look at the lifespan of the Jews born at that time, we see that there are very few still alive today around the world. It has been seventy years up until the year 2018. This fact and the fact that we are now seeing ALL the signs in the world and in mankind, the Lord has shown me that we are in the last of the last days!

~~~~~~

Regarding the Rapture, there are several verses promising that all the believers in Jesus and the Holy Spirit himself will be removed from earth before the seven-year period of Tribulation and Great Tribulation begins. They are found in Revelation 3:10 and in Revelation 4:1.

~~~~~~

This event was also prophesied in 2 Thessalonians 2:6-7, which says *And you know what is holding him (antichrist) back, for he can be revealed only when his time comes. 7 For this lawlessness is already at work secretly, and it will remain secret until the one who is holding it back steps out of the way.* This refers to the Holy Spirit being taken out of the way. Let me explain.

When you are saved (when you receive Jesus as your Savior), the Holy Spirit comes to live inside of you. At your birth, you were born of the flesh. At the time of your salvation, you are "born again" of the Spirit. John 3:5-8 says, *Jesus replied, "I assure you, no one can enter the Kingdom of God without being born of water and the Spirit. 6 Humans can reproduce only human life, but the Holy Spirit gives birth to spiritual life. 7 So don't be surprised when I say, 'You must be born again.' 8 The wind blows wherever it wants. Just as you can hear the wind but can't tell where it comes from or where it is going, so you can't explain how people are born of the Spirit.*

Right now, billions of saved people (believers) walk about the earth, carrying the Holy Spirit within them. When the Rapture takes place, those who have made Jesus the Lord of their lives will be taken out of the world, thus the Holy Spirit will be taken out as well.

~~~†~~~

At this point, I will give you a preview of some of the events that are soon to take place on earth. I recommend that you pick up the Bible and turn to the last book called the Book of Revelation. (I am primarily using the NLT version of the Bible.) It is important that you read the verses in Revelation, so you can learn for yourself what is about to take place on this earth. You can access the Bible on your smart device or read it in book form. The reason it is so important is so that you will receive the blessing found in Revelation 1:3.

I must explain something. Some of the descriptions found in the book of Revelation are literal, some are metaphorical. Once the Rapture takes place, those left behind will have witnessed billions of people simply vanish from the face of the earth! There will be automobiles crashing all over the world; airplanes will fall from the sky. There will be absolute chaos worldwide. People from all walks of life – from doctors, nurses, teachers, engineers, and pilots to construction workers and all other occupations – will be gone! Graves in cemeteries will open, and the dead bodies will be missing! These will be the Christians who have put their faith in Jesus Christ and made him Lord of their lives, who have been taken up to heaven. So, if you find yourself left behind after this event, then you have not received Jesus Christ into your heart as your Savior. All is not lost. You can still receive salvation and go to heaven during this seven-year period known as the Tribulation and Great Tribulation if you accept Jesus as your Savior.

The period between Jesus' death, burial, and resurrection until the Rapture is referred to as the "Age of Grace," whereby He died for you. After the Age of Grace during the seven-year period of the Tribulation and Great Tribulation, you can still be saved for eternity, but you will have to die for Jesus. Because of this event, the world will be a mess! Normal everyday basic functions like shopping for gas and food will be nearly impossible.

This will cause the one world leader to arise to power. In Revelation 6:2, he is known as the antichrist or the beast. He will seemingly have all the answers to the world's problems. He is going to unite everyone, and there will be peace. He will be a mesmerizing figure who will speak with authority. He will start by making peace between Israel and other Arab nations. It will be a seven-year treaty, and the whole world will come together. (This is the one world leader spoken about in Daniel 9:27.) From the date of the signing of this peace treaty, it will be exactly 2,520 days until Jesus Christ will return to earth for His Second Coming.

Next, the third Jewish temple will be built in Jerusalem, and sacrifices and offerings by the Jewish people will begin again. Then the people will be running around saying, we finally have peace and safety! (This is found in 1 Thessalonians 5:3.) This peace will last for three and one-half years, and this world leader will be loved by all mankind. After this three and one-half years of peace, this man – the one world leader – will break the peace treaty, and all hell will literally break loose. He will exalt himself and defy everything godly and every object of worship. He will sit in the new Jewish temple and declare himself God! He will come to do the work of Satan, and he will have counterfeit power, signs, and miracles. He will use every kind of evil deception to fool those on their way to destruction, because they refuse to love and accept the truth that would save them. The people of the earth will be condemned for enjoying evil rather than believing the truth! (Jesus Christ) Satan will now possess the antichrist, and it will be his last attempt to convince everyone on earth that he is the one true God.

~~~☦~~~

The antichrist will align himself with the false prophet. He will be the one world religious leader. Both of these men will perform many signs and miracles. The antichrist will rule over ten kingdoms with ten world leaders. If you go online and look up the Club of Rome you will see the ten kingdoms already laid out on the world map!!! This is how close we are to the end! The antichrist will receive a deadly head wound and live! The one world religious leader will require everyone on earth to receive a mark in their right hand or forehead. It is called the mark of the beast in the Bible. It will contain the number 666 embedded within this mark. If you go online and look up the company called Digital Angel, they manufacture a digital chip the size of a grain of rice that is inserted into your right hand. It has GPS capability and it can store vast amounts of personal data. Whatever the mark they use you will recognize it by this. You will NOT be able to BUY or SELL ANYTHING without it!!! DO NOT RECEIVE THIS MARK OR YOU WILL LOSE YOUR SOUL!!! If you choose to take this mark you will be able to buy food and the basic necessities to survive, but in the end, you will die and go to hell as your punishment. I ask you is it really worth it to be able to survive for an extra three and one-half years of life and then be killed anyway??? He will also set up an image of the antichrist and cause all to worship it. This image will be able to speak. This is found in Revelation 13.

There will then be a great war, famine and plague everywhere. One-fourth of the world's population will die from these three events. This is found in Revelation 6:4-8

You will now witness the earth's greatest ecological disaster. There will be a great earthquake, and the sun will become dark. The moon will become as red as blood, and the stars will fall from the sky. The sky will be rolled up like a scroll, and all the mountains and islands will be moved from their places. On the cover of this book is an image of a nuclear blast with the clouds rolling up into a scroll (a circle). This is found in Revelation 6:12-14.

~~~†~~~

Next, the whole earth will experience the greatest hour of fear. This is found in Revelation 6:15-17.

Next, God will send out 144,000 of His chosen men from the twelve tribes of Israel to preach the Gospel of the Kingdom of Jesus Christ. This is found in Revelation 7:1-8.

Next will be the second war with the earth's greatest fire, and one-third of the earth will be consumed. It will be a nuclear war! One-third of the waters will become polluted and bitter (poisonous) and many people will die from this war and from drinking the water. This is found in Revelation 8:7-11.

~~~†~~~

The Two Witnesses who are God's prophets will now appear and preach in Jerusalem for 1,260 days. If anyone tries to harm them, fire will flash from their mouths and consume their enemies. They will have great power to cause no rain to fall. They will turn the rivers and oceans to blood and cause any kind of plague they choose. When they complete their testimony, the beast (Satan possessing him) will attack and kill them! Their bodies will lay in the main street of Jerusalem for three and one-half days. People around the world will celebrate the deaths of these two men of God! After three and one-half days, God will bring them back to life. The whole world will see it happen on live television, social media, and their cell phones. A terrible earthquake will happen, one-tenth of the city will be destroyed, and seven thousand people will die. After this event everyone will be so terrified, they will fall on their knees and worship the true God, Yahweh! This is found in Revelation 11:1-13.

~~~†~~~

At this time, a remnant of the Jewish people will flee into the wilderness and will be protected by God for 1,260 days. Satan who will now be possessing the antichrist will pursue the Jewish people and try to kill them and wipe them off the map. This is found in Revelation 12:1-17.

~~~†~~~

The next event will be when the 144,000 Jewish men are taken up to heaven. This is found in Revelation 14:1-5.

~~~†~~~

Three angels will now appear. The first will proclaim for all to fear God and give glory to Him! The second will proclaim that Babylon has fallen. The third will declare that anyone who worships the beast or his statue or receives his mark (666) on the forehead or the hand, they will be tormented both day and night forever in the lake of fire! This is found in Revelation 14:6-11.

~~~†~~~

Next will be the earth's greatest epidemic. Malignant sores will break out on everyone who has the mark of the beast or who worshiped the statue of the beast! This is found in Revelation 16:2.

~~~†~~~

Next will be the earth's greatest scorching. The sun will scorch all mankind left alive. They will curse God and not repent of their sins or give Him glory! This is found in Revelation 16:8-9.

~~~†~~~

The earth's greatest plague will be poured out on the throne of the beast, and his kingdom will be plunged into darkness. His subjects will grind their teeth in anguish, curse God, and they will not repent of their evil deeds and turn to God! This is found in Revelation 16:10-11.

~~~~~~

Next will be the earth's greatest invasion. The kings of the east with 200 million troops will march toward the west. The Bible then tells us that three unclean demonic spirits that look like frogs also known as the grey aliens and will gather the armies of the world and march to the valley of Megiddo for the final battle known as the Battle of Armageddon. The remaining people left alive on earth will welcome these aliens and their hybrid Nephilites and they ALL will go to war with the God of Israel who has brought ALL this pain on them!!! I say this to you with absolute certainty, these aliens will appear at this time and make themselves known to mankind! This is found in Revelation 16:12-16.

~~~~~~

Next will be the earth's worst earthquake ever known to mankind. The cities of many nations will become heaps of rubble. Every island and mountain will be leveled. A great hailstorm will drop blocks of ice weighing as much as seventy-five pounds each on the people gathered in the valley of Megiddo! This will cause the blood to flow five feet high for 180 miles. This is found in Revelation 16:18-21.

~~~☦~~~

Now God will judge the false prophet and one world church, the beast, and the ten kingdoms of the world who will rule and reign with the beast during the last three and one-half years. This is found in Revelation 17.

~~~☦~~~

Next will be the fall of Babylon. This is found in Revelation 18.

~~~☦~~~

Jesus will now come back to earth on a white horse with all the saints of heaven with him. Jesus will set his feet down on the Mount of Olives, and the Jewish people will recognize at last that He is their Messiah! He will capture the beast and the false profit and cast them into the lake of fire! He will defeat the armies gathered in the valley of Megiddo by the sharp sword that will come out of the mouth of Jesus which is the word of God!!! This is found in Revelation 19:11-21.

~~~☦~~~

Next an angel from heaven will seize Satan and bound him with a heavy chain and cast him into the bottomless pit for one thousand years. Jesus will now set up his millennial kingdom, and all the saints will rule and reign with him for one thousand years of love and peace! This is found in Revelation 20:1-4.

Once again, I ask you to open the Bible and read the Book of Revelation. I pray that you read it so that you can be spared the pure hell that is coming to the earth in the near future. You do not have to go through all of these horrible events if you except Jesus as your savior now! If not, once it begins, I pray that you will accept the Lord Jesus Christ as your Savior. I pray that I was able to help you understand what is about to happen on the earth. To all my brothers and sisters of the world, grace and peace and love be with you all.

CHAPTER TWELVE
MY FINAL THOUGHTS

I plead the Blood of Jesus over all who have read this book so that you will be protected from the evil one and his demons. In writing this book, I know that I have done my very best to serve my Lord and Savior Jesus Christ. I was placed on this earth at this time for this purpose, and I am so grateful for it. I was created to love and worship my God, and I eagerly do so! If you study the Bible, you will learn just how great and mighty our God truly is! All the chapters in my book reflect His greatness! We sin, but He still loves us so dearly. It is my prayer that ALL mankind will recognize this love He has for us and love and serve Him in return! It is the least we can do! I choose to love and serve you, Father God!

~~~ † ~~~

I am the weakest of the weak. I have shared with you how many times Satan has attacked my body, my mind, and my relationships. My life has been so hard because of all the different attacks he has cursed me with. Throughout the writing of this book, Satan has attacked me with chest pain, nausea, dizziness, and loss of focus!

The Lord chose me to do this work for his glory and his purpose, not mine. God has revealed these secret and hidden truths that I have shared with you. He directed me to different Bible verses and different mentors who helped me in my walk of faith. I am just a simple man, but God saw it was good to use me, "the weak" to lead "the strong."

At some points of my life, the Lord has healed my physical ailments. At other times, He hasn't. I will explain why that is. When you pray to the Lord, He will answer in one of three ways. The first is, He will answer your prayer outright. You will receive your request. The second is, He will give you the strength by the power of the Holy Spirit to get you through whatever you are going through. The third is, He will take you out of the situation and have mercy on you. In some cases, for instance if you have a severe illness, in his mercy He will let you pass away. There are times in our lives when we have loved ones who are terminally ill. We are not ready to lose them. Most times we do anything we can to prolong their life, thus their suffering, because we are not ready for them to pass away. This is when as a Christian, you can make it through this time in your life with peace. Yes, you will grieve, but because of your solid faith in Jesus Christ, you can also rejoice because you know that you will be reunited with them again if they too are saved. You are saved by the blood of Jesus, you do not have to fear death! In 2 Corinthians 5:8 it says, *Yes, we are fully confident, and we would rather be away from these earthly bodies, for then we will be at home with the Lord.* Once you are saved, you have nothing to fear, not even death. If you are saved by the blood of Jesus and you were to die today, then you would go to heaven to be with Jesus. Hallelujah! This is what faith is ALL ABOUT. Putting your total trust in Jesus Christ will make your life abundant and the time of your death peaceful. None of us have the choice of how He will act on our behalf. The one thing you can absolutely count on is that He will do what is best for you, but it will be HIS will for you.

~~~✝~~~

When you put your faith in God, He will test you! This testing is necessary for growth in your faith walk, known as walking out your salvation. Philippians 2:12 says, *Dear friends, you always followed my instructions when I was with you. And now that I am away, it is even more important. Work hard to show the results of your salvation, obeying God with deep reverence and fear.*

I have told you about my visit to heaven with Jesus. I held the hand of the Creator. Everything I saw in heaven was confirmed in the Bible and through science. I was sent to hell to give a first-hand account of it. I was then shown in the Bible what hell was. I have proven that the Bible contains prophecies about world history. I have proven to you that God exists, both through the Bible and through science and nature. I have given you my testimony about the attacks from Satan and the miracles that have happened to me in my life. I have proven the existence of the battles we face in our mind and lives. I have proven the existence of the supernatural in our world and that evil exists. I have shown you through Bible verses and world history that Jesus Christ did indeed live on this earth, and that He is the Son of God, our Savior. I have shown you the meaning of life and how we are to love each other.

In the previous chapter, I have shown you what will happen on earth in the near future. I believe that I have proven beyond any reasonable person's doubt, that the Bible is the one and only true book of God's Word! It is the Living Word of God! To further intrigue you, there is a book called, "The Bible Code." Eliyahu Rips, a mathematician who co-authored it, found that hidden in the text of the Bible were messages (ELS or Equidistant Letter Sequence) that could only be revealed through the use of a computer program that correctly predicts specific people and events in world history. It contains hidden messages about Shakespeare and about the murders of John F. Kennedy and Yitzhak Rabin. It also has hidden messages about the two space shuttle tragedies, about 911, and about many more world events that have happened or will happen. Go online and research the information about the Bible Code. Now to my point. The Lord has shown me that my name is encrypted within this Bible code. It was preordained by God for me to have all the life experiences that I have shared with you, and for me to write them down in this book. He has shown me that this book will be published, and people will read it worldwide. I will also speak about it in churches and other public events. I am so grateful that God allowed me to use the technology (that Satan himself devised to deceive the whole world) against him, to reveal the truth about him and his demons!

Now I want to share with you what will happen in the coming months and years. You will see even more extreme major hurricanes (category 3 and higher), typhoons, and massive tornados. Some of them will happen in places where they are not common! You will see major flooding worldwide as thunderstorms will produce all-time record amounts of rainfall in places like India and the United States! In some parts of the world, including the western United States, Africa, Australia, and Portugal, you will see even more extreme droughts and wild fires. You will see major snow storms with all-time record amounts of snow in many parts of England and in the United States where it is not normal to receive these heavy amounts of snow. There will be even more earthquakes, tsunamis, and volcanic eruptions worldwide that will increase in frequency and severity leading up to the end! You will see massive sinkholes worldwide. There will also be civil unrest worldwide as people rise up against the rulers of their countries. YES, the globe is warming! It is my belief that God will use this warming as a punishment on all people of the world for not taking better care of the earth. The Democrats and Socialists will finally receive what they are asking for, once the one world leader comes into power. He will offer them world peace and climate control, and he will be an all-inclusive kind of leader for the first three and one-half years! Once the Rapture of the Christian Church happens, the Christians – I believe including most Republicans – will no longer be on this earth. Thus, leaving those believing in Democratic principles and all unbelieving people in the world behind! He will lead you like cattle to the slaughter, straight to hell! In the second three and one-half years, he will TURN ON YOU. These events will happen. I am warning you now so when you see it happen, you will know that I have been sent by God to warn you of these world events that are soon to commence.

It is important to note that the Rapture and the Second Coming of Christ are two separate events. In the Rapture, Jesus will descend on the clouds, and all his believers all over the world will meet him in the air. This will be a supernatural event, and it will not be visible to the nonbelieving people of the world! You will see the effects of it worldwide. After the seven-year period of the Tribulation and the Great Tribulation, Jesus will return to earth, setting his feet on the Mount of Olives in Jerusalem. This when the Jewish people will recognize that Jesus is their Messiah! He is the Messiah for ALL mankind!

I must warn all the people who have hatred toward the Jewish people to turn away from your hate, or you will see the wrath of God come upon you!!! Please accept Jesus Christ as your Savior now or get prepared to face the most horrific time in the history of mankind! All the pain and hardship that we experience is caused by Satan! He is the reason the world is like it is with murders, drug use, and child abuse. The list goes on and on! If you need to hate someone, hate Satan! God is not responsible for any of this pain!

Recently, God has shown me in a dream that I was running a race. There were thousands of people in the race, but they were only walking in a long and winding line. As I ran past the long line of people, I came around a corner and saw a finish line with white tape across the road and the word FINISH written on the road. I was only ten feet away from reaching it. I have contemplated this dream and have come to the conclusion that my race is almost over. All the other people I saw in the race represent mankind. The end is near. So, during the time I have left in this life, I will be speaking to anyone and everyone who will listen to my warnings of just how close the end is – how close the return of Jesus Christ is!

I will leave you with this final Bible verse. In Matthew 16:26 it says, *And what do you benefit if you gain the whole world, but lose your own soul? Is anything worth more than your soul?* Stop living your life for material gain. Ever since you were a child, you have been taught that you must be successful. You have been taught to win at all cost and to gain all you can in this life. This is wrong! You should live your life for God! We are only here on this earth a short time. It is like a second compared to all of eternity! Love your God with all your heart, all your soul, all your mind, and all your strength! And love your fellow man as you love yourself. Give more of your wealth to the poor and needy. I live my life by these truths. I love and serve my God first, then my family and friends and my country. I am nothing special. Everyone is called by God to love and serve him. The choice is whether or not you will choose to do so. Choose Jesus Christ and you choose eternal life! The one thing that I have learned about the Word of God is that if it says that something happened in the past, it did! If it says something will happen in the future, it will! You can bet your eternal life on it! Our earthly life will soon pass, but only a life lived for Jesus will last.

Please contemplate everything I have revealed to you in my book. You can be part of this ministry and help me reach the lost people in this world. When you are finished reading it, please go on social media and recommend this book or give a copy to someone in your family, your circle of friends, your co-workers – someone you know who needs the gift of salvation and a relationship with Jesus Christ. You can order additional copies of my book exclusively on Amazon. It is available in paperback or e-book form. It is being made available to many countries of the world in many languages. If you would like me to come and speak at your church or other public function, you can contact me at thebloodofjesussavesall@gmail.com. We cannot let one person be lost forever to Satan! I pray to the Lord God Almighty that those of you who have read this book will receive the grace, peace, and knowledge that only comes from the Lord Jesus Christ. Call out to Jesus, and he will answer you. To all my brothers and sisters of the world, I love you all. May God bless you all. Come quickly, Lord Jesus!

A prophetic word from my sister in Christ, Sharilee Rudolph

Heaven's Stairs

While waking up 11/4/18 I saw the picture of the Bride walking the stairs to Heaven and this is the prophetic Word that came.

You walk the stairs to Heaven by way of trial and tests. Each step you take washed in Amazing Grace! The way is long and narrow, paved with suffering. The trials, the tests, only try and prove you in refiner's fire. So take the stairway in confidence! The blood applied covers you! The robe of Righteousness you wear! Tears are in His bottle, your eyes dried by the love you share – The Holy love of the Bridegroom, keeps you walking in merriment! As the joys of Heaven are seen by all – who on the savior do call!

Breathe the air of Heaven, the life of God in you! In this earth suit filled with Glory, one day you will exchange – the stairway leads to Heaven – each step was worth it all! From Glory to Glory He is changing me! Now I see the land so bright! So Holy! I hear the angels sing! The steps of suffering and pain are behind me! The joy of the Lord is strength! The air of Heaven – Oh how clean and bright! The door is shut and I am in! Jesus my Savior! Jesus my all! – has the key to my heart. He unlocked the chains, took away all sin! His Bride made ready! Now will dance and live with Him!

O Jesus precious Jesus! The stairs were hard to climb – but worth it all. As I see your smile, your joy is mine and mine is you! O the joy of Heaven! Till that day I will walk in faith, eyes to see beyond the earthly veil – made for Heaven – I see the pearly gates!

As I wait for that day, at the altar I will dwell, to pour out my love – to worship the Lamb King! To my Heavenly Bridegroom I give you all Glory, all Honor, and Praise. At the Altar of surrender you begin to climb, each act of surrender, His Glory is formed in you! You are transformed! At the altar to worship with clean hands and pure heart the journey begins – see the love of Jesus on the path you take – yield to God and rest in Him.

Thy Kingdom Come! Thy Will be done! Is the shout of victory!! The Warrior Bride beholds the Bridegroom and the wedding is soon to be!

Made in the USA
Columbia, SC
02 April 2019